"Timeless Church is solid. It notes that the bedrock bas[...] in the first century should also guide it in the twenty-first century. Doctrine, community, prayer, giving, and evangelism never grow old or go out of style. Biblically faithful and extremely practical, it will serve the Lord's churches well."

—Daniel L. Akin, president, Southeastern Baptist Theological Seminary

"The twenty-first-century church has many questions, and the book of Acts is a great place to look for answers. I'm thankful for my friends and their engaging book *Timeless Church: Five Lessons from Acts.* Herein you will not only learn more about the early church, but you will also learn what God has to say to your church."

—Jason K. Allen, president, Midwestern Baptist Theological Seminary

"In *Timeless Church,* McClendon and Lockhart demonstrate a clear and biblical understanding of what makes church, well . . . church! And they do so in a way that reminds you of the relevancy of the church in today's age. In simple, yet profound ways, they speak to the elements of church that allows it (us) to function as a glorious reflection of God's character and love for his people. The idea expressed in Jer 32:38, 'They will be my people, and I will be their God' (CSB), comes shining through, and you will be encouraged."

—Doug Bischoff, Next Generations Minister, Houston's First Baptist Church, Houston, TX

"Adam and Jared have written a great book with tools to build a church and present a model that has been multiplied over all the generations. I have served in and with the local church for more than forty years. God says in Matthew that he will build his church. The book of Acts is the model for his church and what the components of his church should be. Today, churches often want to do something different to stand out, but God set the pattern in Acts, and it has never changed. Lessons learned from these foundational components of a local church are tested, tried, and true."

—Tracy Hipps, executive director, Christian Service Mission, Birmingham, AL

"Nothing jeopardizes the growth of a new convert like neglecting the local church. *Timeless Church* encourages the new believer (and reminds the old) to seek a church that is faithful to the gospel, the Scriptures, and the family of God. Lockhart and McClendon write with accessible prose as they introduce the tenets of ecclesiology. We would do well to put *Timeless Church* in the hands of every new believer."

—Matthew Kimbrough, assistant professor of theology, Southwest Baptist University

"*Timeless Church* is a timeless message the modern church desperately needs. This inspiring, challenging, and practical study of the bare-knuckle basics of the church in the book of Acts helps all churches of today drill to the core of being who Jesus has called us to be for his glory. You won't regret a minute of reading this faithful work."

—Kenny Qualls, senior pastor, First Baptist Church, Arnold, MO

"*Timeless Church* is a remarkable book that was written to help you think about church in life-changing ways. The approach to glean lessons about the church from the book of Acts is not necessarily new, but I have not read a book that provides so much helpful insight in considering what a church should be. In addition, the book provides helpful ways to engage with the material by providing group questions and five days of devotions at the end of each section. This is a tremendous way to engage both the book of Acts and one another in serious discussion of the purpose of a church."

—David Talley, professor of Old Testament, Talbot School of Theology, Biola University

"McClendon and Lockhart help us to see how the church in the book of Acts is an example for your local church. Amply illustrated and immensely practical, *Timeless Church* provides several prescriptions, which, if followed, would be a boon to the health of any church. The discussion questions and devotional sections that follow each chapter make the book an excellent candidate for either individual reading or small-group study."

—Donald S. Whitney, professor of biblical spirituality and associate dean of the school of theology, The Southern Baptist Theological Seminary

"Adam McClendon and Jared Lockhart brilliantly articulate the five foundational characteristics of the early church found in the book of Acts to show why these foundational characteristics are still just as important for the spiritual awakening for today's church. Their model is a timeless reminder of the lessons that the church, found in the book of Acts, organically utilized to grow and to empower the believers to advance the gospel and influence the world through prayer and the Word of God."

—Dante D. Wright, pastor, Sweet Home—The Pinnacle of Praise, Round Rock, TX

TIMELESS

CHURCH

Five Lessons from Acts

TIMELESS

CHURCH

P. Adam McClendon & Jared E. Lockhart

B&H
ACADEMIC
NASHVILLE, TENNESSEE

Jared:

*To my parents, Barry and Jonavieve Lockhart, thank you
for faithfully passing on the good deposit of the gospel and
raising me in the community of God's people.*

In loving memory of Barry D. Lockhart (1963–2019)

Adam:

*Thank you, Springhill Baptist Church, for allowing these truths
to be studied, taught, cultivated, and practiced. You are a special
place, and I'm privileged to have been part of your story.*

*Thank you, Bedrock Community Church, for living
these characteristics out and demonstrating an
unwavering confidence in God's Word and ways.*

CONTENTS

INTRODUCTION

If you have ever bought a piece of furniture from a big-box store like IKEA, then you are familiar with the detailed set of instructions that come with the product. The multipage document containing them is always prominently placed in the packaging and provides a step-by-step approach to putting the furniture together. The instructions vary on how intelligible they actually are; but on the whole, they provide a detailed picture for assembly.

The book you hold in your hands is not like those instructions. This is not an instruction manual for doing church. This is not a how-to church book. This is not a detailed, step-by-step approach that will explain all there is to know about the church or all there is to know about doing church. It is more of an overview than a step-by-step guide. We have pulled out five foundational characteristics of the early church that are evidenced in the book of Acts, and we have sought to show why they are just as important for the modern church seeking to be faithful followers of Jesus Christ. This application-based approach flows from the conviction that the New Testament, and particularly Acts, does not merely provide us with a description of how the church formed and grew, but those writings provide us with God's prescription for how he desires for his church to function for all time. Thus, if the Bible provides a structure for his church, it is imperative that we know and conform to that structure over and against our pragmatic tendencies.

We wrote this book because we love the church of our Lord Jesus and desire to see (1) others grow in their love for the church, (2) more people faithfully living out the call of Christ in their church communities, and, (3) overall, we seek to make much of Jesus, who considers the church his bride. Know that we have been praying for you. We pray that God uses this book in your life and that he uses it to build and edify his church.

Maybe you are a faithful churchgoer and want to refresh your understanding of the church. Maybe you have been attending church for years, but have some doubt as to why. Maybe you are a small group or church leader and need to get back to basics. Maybe you are a new believer and want to know more about the church. Maybe you are not a Christian and want to understand what church is for Christians. No matter who you are or what your motive is for picking up this book, we hope to point you to Jesus and honor his bride as we lay out some of the basics about the church. With that being said, this book is specifically designed to aid those new to their faith in Christ, or those who have never gone deep in that relationship, in considering the church's purpose in God's plan and in their own lives. Church leaders, small group facilitators, and church planters can also greatly benefit from the discussion in this book. This can be a good resource to help you in discussing and leading others through their questions about the church and even to prepare your own heart and mind for consideration of foundational ecclesiological (that is, church-related) issues.

The hope is that this book provides a foundation that can be built upon by your church gathering. We do not answer all the questions or cover all the passages that have relevant, even important things to say about the church. This is an overview of some of the most important characteristics; however, we have also included many practical illustrations and application points. The goal is for this book to be a useful resource. You will find at the end of each chapter some discussion questions along with a five-day devotional. Be sure to check out the appendix for some additional resources.

While it is not essential, we suggest you read this book with others. Your experience will be heightened by having a community around you to discuss, think, and bounce ideas off of. Small groups may want to consider walking through this book as well. We have done our best to include the text of Scripture because that is where spiritual power lies: not in our words, but in the Word of God. Do not allow this book or any other to replace your time in the Word; allow this to push you deeper into the Word of God.

CHAPTER 1

CONFESSING CHURCH:
We Believe in Jesus

Grounding all activity in the central confession of Jesus as the Messiah was a central characteristic of the early church as detailed in the book of Acts.

> And they *devoted themselves to the apostles' teaching* and the fellowship, to the breaking of bread and the prayers. And awe came upon every soul, and many wonders and signs were being done through the apostles. And all who believed were together and had all things in common. And they were selling their possessions and belongings and distributing the proceeds to all, as any had need. And day by day, attending the temple together and breaking bread in their homes, they received their food with glad and generous hearts, praising God and having favor with all the people. And the Lord added to their number day by day those who were being saved. (Acts 2:42–47)

What Makes a Church?

When the Lord got a hold on my life, I (Adam) began attending a church as the result of a friend's invitation. Looking back these many years later,

3

I realize that I unintentionally viewed church as more of a department store than a place of worship. The central question lurking behind all my observations was, "Does it have what I need?" I was a consumer seeking to receive, ignorant of the call to serve and love others in community. My time needed to be well spent and my needs met. Shortly after I began attending this church, it became a refuge: a home away from home. A love for the people blossomed in my heart. I soon invited others to church, to join me in this wonderful journey. However, my invitation to them focused around individual preferences, like I was pointing out trinkets at a sales booth. I promoted my church to others based on how it would accommodate them, serve them, and fulfill them. I was too young and immature to think past this approach to bigger questions, like these:

- Does this church proclaim biblical beliefs and doctrine?
- Does it have a biblical leadership structure?
- Does it foster and celebrate biblical community?
- Does it engage culture with the gospel?
- Does it make much of Jesus and challenge people to live in obedience to him?

By fixating on the programs and services of the church, as good and helpful as they were, I missed what it means for the church to be the church.

These many years later, as I talk to people, coach and encourage leaders within various denominations, and work with parachurch organizations, I find we tend to promote dynamic preaching, a meaningful worship experience, good programming for children, and a solid youth ministry. Now, do not get me wrong: I hope that our churches have all of these. Yet in the midst of these more experience-oriented programs, we must not lose sight of the central confession that defines and determines a Christian church. What makes a Christian church is not just its activity in gathering but its confession of specific truths. This word *confession* is not one commonly used in our culture, but it is an important concept that makes all the difference. Confession is central to church, and without it, a true Christian church cannot exist. Additionally, when this confession is in place, it grounds and brings purpose to all other activities, programs, and experiences—but we are getting ahead of ourselves. First, we must discuss what is meant by the word *confession* and why it is so important.

Confessing Love

My wife, Adrienne, and I met when I was fifteen. Here is the story of how we did, and how I came to love this amazing woman. At fifteen I was dysfunctional on many levels. I was dealing with some deep emotional scars from so much that had happened in my life already. I was even wrestling with whether I wanted to live. One night, I was in a horrible car accident that should have taken my life. God used that event to give me a desire not just to live, but to find and live out his purpose for my life. I began searching as never before.

A couple of weeks later, sitting in class at school, a young man named Chad invited me to church. Chad and his parents began picking me up and taking me to the Wednesday night youth group. This place was safe and quickly became my refuge. That first Wednesday night, I walked in wearing my cool leather jacket and reeking of cologne—a little really does go a long way, but I just felt a little more would go a little further. Frankly, I was ridiculous. But that night, several people, including Adrienne, took time to talk to me. They genuinely seemed to want to get to know me, to hear my story, and to encourage me in my walk with God. It was like precious ointment on my wounded soul.

Adrienne, two other students, and I quickly became the best of friends. They were regularly picking me up for church, and we were all together every weekend, with rare exceptions. These people were my family during this time, and God began a great work in my life. Through this youth group, our amazing youth pastor, his wife, and these friends, I sensed a call into full-time vocational ministry.

Adrienne and I had a great friendship during this season of my life. We never dated; we simply cherished our friendship and challenged each other to cling to Christ. She was one year ahead of me in school. After graduating, she went to college in Tennessee, while two months into my senior year, I became convinced that the Lord was leading me to serve in the military as a missionary. One evening right before leaving for the military, while Adrienne was home visiting for the summer, I was hanging out at her house. As we were enjoying each other's company, suddenly I looked deep into her eyes and realized for the first time that I saw her as more than a friend. That evening, I kissed her. Shortly after that night, I left for boot camp, and Adrienne began her sophomore year of college. We never spoke of the kiss.

Right after boot camp, my youth pastor, who also worked with the college and young adults in our church, invited me to a college retreat. I was especially excited when I discovered Adrienne was going to be there too. That weekend, as we all hung out and walked, I held her hand, still never mentioning the kiss. Avoiding the issue was not going to fly with her, however. She wanted to know what I was doing and where we were with our relationship. I remember saying something like, "I care deeply for you and cherish our friendship, but I can't go further. I'm not going to date you unless I know you are the woman I'm going to marry."

Then, with amazing confidence, she looked at me and said, "Well, I already know I'm going to marry you."

I laughed out loud and responded, "No, you don't."

"Yes, I do," she replied calmly.

"Well, I don't know that."

What she said next shocked me even more: "That's okay. I'll wait on you."

About three months later, I was in a military training school. I could not stop thinking and praying about our conversation. I remember thinking about the type of woman I wanted to be with when I was seventy years old, after fifty years of marriage. *Adrienne is* exactly *the type of woman I want to be with*, I thought, so *why should I keep looking for what I've already found?* It was then that I committed and decided to confess my love for her and ask her to be my girlfriend. In doing so, it was as if I was asking her to marry me one day, because that purpose was behind it.

What is the point of this story, other than providing a lot of detail about my past? The point is this: a moment came, through a variety of divinely directed circumstances, when I realized my genuine love and commitment to Adrienne, and I confessed it to her.

What Does "Confession" Actually Mean?

Confession is more than just silent belief. It is the expression and proclamation of beliefs for an individual or a collective group of people. A confession is proclaimed both privately and publicly. In confessing my love for Adrienne, I was proclaiming what I believed to be true. A confession can either be written or spoken, but more than that, a confession must be believed and lived. Its truth must show in the way the one who confesses it lives.

The church has confessed her beliefs in written documents since her inception in the first-century AD. These confessions are found in the writings of individuals (such as the apostle Paul and early church fathers) and in the writings of groups and councils (such as the First London Baptist Confession and the Westminster Confession of Faith).[1] Early in the history of the church, a number of doctrines arose that set apart individuals as Christians and groups as Christian churches.[2] Among these doctrines were a biblical understanding of the Trinity, that Christ was born of a virgin, and that the Bible is the Word of God.[3] These doctrines, among others, were seen as most distinctive of Christianity and among the most essential biblical doctrines. Affirming these accepted beliefs set individuals apart as orthodox Christians; however, even before these, there was and still is today a confession even more central and foundational, as it has been central since the beginning of Jesus's ministry.

This confession was at the heart of Jesus's interactions with his own disciples. This most central confession of the church is found in Acts 5:42: "And every day, in the temple and from house to house, they did not cease teaching and preaching that *the Christ is Jesus*." This central confession that "Jesus is the Christ" is the root to the trunk of the early church and is found all over the book of Acts (e.g., 2:22–36; 3:13–26; 4:10–12; 5:42; 8:12; 10:34–43; 11:17; 16:31; 17:2–3; 18:5, 28; 20:21; 24:24). Acts is an important text for understanding the central confession of the early church because this book outlines the movement of the Spirit of God in and through the disciples as they take the message and Spirit of Jesus to the ends of the earth.[4] The central confession that Jesus is the Christ is what animates the disciples and pushes them to action: actions that are documented in the book of Acts. This truth that Jesus is the Christ is the central confession of the church. The Scriptures lay this out quite clearly. In Matthew 16 we read:

> He said to them, "But who do you say that I am?" Simon Peter replied, "You are the Christ, the Son of the living God." And Jesus answered him, "Blessed are you, Simon Bar-Jonah! For flesh and blood has not revealed this to you, but my Father who is in heaven. And I tell you, you are Peter, and on this rock I will build my church, and the gates of hell shall not prevail against it." (vv. 15–18)

---

[1] The First London Baptist Confession was penned in 1644, and the Westminster Confession of Faith was penned in 1646. Some other influential and well-known written corporate confessions include the Reformed Heidelberg Catechism of 1563 and, more recently, the Baptist New Hampshire Confession of Faith of 1833.

[2] The word *doctrine* simply refers to a belief (right or wrong) that is held by a particular group.

[3] This list is by no means exhaustive of the core beliefs of the Christian church.

[4] Acts 1:8 reads, "But you will receive power when the Holy Spirit has come upon you, and you will be my [Jesus's] witnesses in Jerusalem and in all Judea and Samaria, and to the end of the earth." The book of Acts is an unfolding of this prophetic statement by Jesus. It presents a historical record of Spirit-empowered saints taking the confession regarding Jesus as the Christ to the ends of the earth and seeing masses of people repent of their sins and be born again by placing their personal faith in Jesus as their Lord and Savior.

Peter here clearly and succinctly confesses Jesus as the Christ, the Messiah of Israel, but what is most important about this passage is Jesus's reaction. Jesus affirms this truth wholeheartedly. He may as well have said, "You are absolutely right! That is correct!" However, notice that he goes beyond simply acknowledging Peter's confession as theologically correct; Jesus suggests that this confession is the foundation of the church. Jesus as the Christ is the truth on which the church is to be built. It is the foundational truth that buttresses all others for the people of God and all creation. But, what exactly does that mean?

The title "Christ" means "Anointed One." The title is applied to Jesus and is used to show that Jesus is the promised Jewish Messiah. The Messiah is the anticipated Old Testament figure who is to be the fulfillment of the promises of God. The promise of the Messiah goes all the way back to Gen 3:15. After Adam and Eve rebel against God by disobeying his command not to eat the fruit of the tree of the knowledge of good and evil, there are consequences. Among other things, they have to leave the goodness of Eden, but there is also a great promise. God says to the snake, "I will put enmity between you and the woman, and between your offspring and her offspring; he shall bruise your head, and you shall bruise his heel" (v. 15). This promised one will defeat evil forever, but in the process the snake will bite his heel.

Later in the book of Genesis, God (eventually) chooses a man named Abraham through whose descendants the world will be blessed. The implication is that the Messiah will be the preeminent one among those descendants. Soon the narrative winds its way to one of those descendants, Judah. God promises that a king will come from his line, one who will unite the whole world and under whose reign there will be peace and prosperity. This is the Messiah.

In time, a great man from the line of Judah becomes king. Though he is described as a man after God's own heart (1 Sam 13:14), David fails and sins. He is not the one.

As the story of Israel—the nation descended from Abraham—continues, each successive generation of kings seems more wicked than the last, until rival kingdoms take over and Israel is reduced to a sort of vassal state. In fact, at this point, the nation goes into exile, and for a time there are no more kings to fulfill the promise. It seems the plan of God has been thwarted. But prophets during this time keep talking about the promise, reminding the people that God is faithful and he will provide the foretold king. One prophet in particular speaks about the coming Messiah and his defeat of death. Isaiah seems to suggest that the Messiah himself will die, then resurrect, and as a result of his own fatal wound (that Gen 3:15 prophesied), he will be able to heal others of the darkness and sin within them (Isaiah 52–53). The canon of the Old Testament closes, and this king still has not come.

The New Testament opens with Jesus as the central character, and the Gospel writers do all they can to show us the true identity of this God-man. He is the promised one, the Messiah. We learn that he is of the line of Abraham, Judah, and David. He begins to cleanse people of the evil effects of the fall by healing disease and forgiving sin. He is the promised Deliverer, Savior, and King (Isa 9:6–7; 53:5–6; Dan 7:13–14; Luke 2:11). He is the one who will rule justly, as prophesied in the Davidic covenant (1 Chr 7:11–14). He is the perfect human, the perfect King, and the one who will save and deliver his people—not from foreign occupying armies, but from the corruption of sin and the finality of death. As this act of the story begins to be triumphant, Jesus starts telling his closest followers that he must die, but that through this death he will truly master death for the whole world. Jesus is, in fact, crucified and rises again three days later. This is the central event of the New Testament, the Bible, and all of human history. Since this perfect King died the painful death of a criminal, some assumed him to be a failed revolutionary. But this too was prophesied. The prophet Isaiah says of him:

> He was oppressed, and he was afflicted, yet he opened not his mouth; like a lamb that is led to the slaughter, and like a sheep that before its shearers is silent, so he opened not his mouth. . . . Out of the anguish of his soul he shall see and be satisfied, by his knowledge shall the righteous one, my servant, make many to be accounted righteous, and he shall bear their iniquities. Therefore I will divide him a portion with the many, and he shall divide the spoil with the strong, because he poured out his soul to death and was numbered with the transgressors; yet he bore the sin of many, and makes intercession for the transgressors. (Isa 53:7, 11–12)

Evidenced in this passage and others like it is the truth that Jesus is a King who not only rules justly for his people, but he also dies on their behalf. He is the crucified one. The kingdom of God was to be established by the Messiah through his fulfillment of the law and bearing the judgment for sin on behalf of those who would trust in him. Jesus, as the Messiah, lived a perfect human life to fulfill the law and died on a Roman cross as the sacrifice for the sins of those who would trust in him for salvation. The rest of the New Testament, then, expounds this event and shows that when we are united to Christ by faith, he heals us and we can invite others in to experience the healing of the King as well.

To the surprise of the Jews, Jesus is not just the Jewish Messiah; he is the Savior, Deliverer, and rightful King of the whole world. That is the message the apostles preached (Acts 2:42) and the message that unifies the church. The body of Christ is to be united around the truth that Jesus as the Christ lived a perfect life, died a sacrificial death, rose to life, ascended to heaven, and presently rules as King of a kingdom that is even now breaking into this world. Furthermore, one day, he will return to establish that kingdom in its fullness, gather his people into that kingdom, and destroy his enemies (1 Cor 15:22–28). That has always been the central confession around which all preaching, outreach, and fellowship were built. Even Peter, one of Jesus's closest disciples and a Jew who followed the law, was confronted with the radical, universal, and essential nature of this confession.

> So Peter opened his mouth and said: "Truly I understand that God shows no partiality, but in every nation anyone who fears him and does what is right is acceptable to him. As for the word that he sent to Israel, preaching good news of peace through Jesus Christ (he is Lord of all), you yourselves know what happened throughout all Judea, beginning from Galilee after the baptism that John proclaimed: how God anointed Jesus of Nazareth with the Holy Spirit and with power. He went about doing good and healing all who were oppressed by the devil, for God was with him. And we are witnesses of all that he did both in the country of the Jews and in Jerusalem. They put him to death by hanging him on a tree, but God raised him on the third day and made him to appear, not to all the people but to us who had been chosen by God as witnesses, who ate and drank with him after he rose from the dead. And he commanded us to preach to the people and to testify that he is the one appointed by God to be judge of the living and the dead. To him all the prophets bear witness that everyone who believes in him receives forgiveness of sins through his name." (Acts 10:34–43)

Peter laid out the confession of the church in this passage. He proclaimed that God's plan is for both the Jews and the Gentiles. This plan was for God's sent Savior and Son to be crucified on a cross, raised from death, and then to appear to witnesses, who would confess that all who believe in him are forgiven of their sins. That was Peter's confession. That was the confession of the early church. And that is our confession still today as followers of Jesus the Christ. What is our confession fundamentally? Jesus is Lord.

This is what that means:

- We confess that we cannot fulfill the requirements of the law of God.
- We confess that we are inadequate.
- We confess that we are sinful.
- We confess that we need more than self-help, moralistic teaching, or therapy.
- We confess that Jesus is the Christ, the Messiah.
- We confess that this Christ is sufficient.
- We confess that this Christ is glorious.
- We confess that this Christ, the Son of God, came and lived, died and rose again, thus fulfilling the requirements of the law on our behalf and providing us with forgiveness from all our sin. He is coming again to claim his children as his own and to judge the living and the dead.
- We confess that all who place their faith in the atoning work of Jesus are redeemed and born again.

Because of what Christ has done, this confession matters for us both as individuals and as a believing community collectively. Why? It is true that because of his life, death, and resurrection we can each have a relationship with God individually. But this confession matters collectively as the people of God gather together corporately because it is only in the context of the church that the new covenant God made with us makes sense (Jer 31:31–34; 1 Cor 11:25–26; Hebrews 8).[5]

In fact, we are only the church as a group. You are not the church; I am not the church. The people of God meeting together, worshiping together, confessing Jesus, and reorienting our hearts toward God together are the church. We, as God's people (even more important than we as individuals), have a relationship with God. I (Jared) have heard it said that the church is the gospel

---

[5]   The Bible consistently speaks of various covenants God has made with his people. While the majority of covenants mentioned in the Old Testament are initially addressed to an individual (such as Abraham, Moses, and David), they contain corporate promises intended for the people of God as a whole. In the midst of this Old Testament covenant context, God declared that he would establish a new covenant with his people (Jer 31:31–34). This new covenant establishes and defines the collective people of God as they live in relationship with God. For an extensive resource on the establishment of the kingdom of God through covenant, see Peter J. Gentry and Stephen J. Wellum, *Kingdom through Covenant: A Biblical-Theological Understanding of the Covenants* (Wheaton, IL: Crossway, 2018).

personified in community. In this community, all elements of his redeeming mission are seen worked out.[6] God relates to both individuals and people groups, but the relationship he has with his church is more vibrant and full than the relationship that any one of us individually can have with God apart from the rest of his body (see Eph 4:1–16). The apostle Peter says it this way:

> As you come to him, a living stone rejected by men but in the sight of God chosen and precious, you yourselves like living stones are being built up as a spiritual house, to be a holy priesthood, to offer spiritual sacrifices acceptable to God through Jesus Christ. For it stands in Scripture:

> > "Behold, I am laying in Zion a stone,
> > a cornerstone chosen and precious,
> > and whoever believes in him will not be put to shame."

> So the honor is for you who believe, but for those who do not believe,

> > "The stone that the builders rejected
> > has become the cornerstone,"

> and

> > "A stone of stumbling,
> > and a rock of offense."

---

[6]   For more on the gospel personified in community and the redemption of God worked out therein, see Joseph Hellerman, *When the Church Was a Family: Recapturing Jesus' Vision for Authentic Christian Community* (Nashville: B&H, 2009); and Dietrich Bonhoeffer, *Life Together: The Classic Exploration of Christian Community* (New York: HarperCollins, 1954). One example of God's redemption being worked out in community that Bonhoeffer discusses is the practice of the confession of sin. He says,

In confession [of sin] there takes place a breakthrough to community. Sin wants to be alone with people. It takes them away from the community. The more lonely people become, the more destructive the power of sin over them. The more deeply they become entangled in it, the more unholy is their loneliness. Sin wants to remain unknown. It shuns the light. In the darkness of what is left unsaid sin poisons the whole being of a person. This can happen in the midst of a pious community. In confession the light of the gospel breaks into the darkness and closed isolation of the heart. Sin must be brought into the light. What is unspoken is said openly and confessed. All that is secret and hidden comes to light. It is a hard struggle until the sin crosses one's lips in confession. But God breaks down gates of bronze and cuts through bars of iron (Ps. 107:16). Since the confession of sin is made in the presence of another Christian, the last stronghold of self-justification is abandoned. The sinner surrenders, giving up all evil, giving the sinner's heart to God and finding the forgiveness of all one's sin in the community of Jesus Christ and other Christians. Sin that has been spoken and confessed has lost all of its power. It has been revealed and judged as sin. It can no longer tear apart the community. (Bonhoeffer, 112–13)

They stumble because they disobey the word, as they were destined to do.

But you are a chosen race, a royal priesthood, a holy nation, a people for his own possession, that you may proclaim the excellencies of him who called you out of darkness into his marvelous light. Once you were not a people, but now you are God's people; once you had not received mercy, but now you have received mercy.

Beloved, I urge you as sojourners and exiles to abstain from the passions of the flesh, which wage war against your soul. (1 Pet 2:4–11)

In this passage, Peter draws from Old Testament language to present Jesus the Messiah as the living cornerstone of this new building—the new temple made of other living stones. We as members of the church are the other living stones mentioned in this passage. Notice the community-oriented language used here. As a part of this spiritual house, we together are to be a holy nation, a chosen race, a royal priesthood, and a people for God's own possession.[7] G. K. Beale wrote, "The very being of the church as witnesses of an invisible temple conveys the presence of God to others."[8] It is in this way that we share in the presence of God with fellow believers and mediate his presence even to unbelievers. This is why there is supreme value in the corporate nature of the church of God. Our mission demands it. We must confess Christ as Lord as individuals, yes, but it becomes even more important and impactful when we confess together that King Jesus is Messiah, Lord, and Savior.

The Confession of the Church Defines the Church

This confession regarding the person and work of Jesus makes and defines a Christian church. Throughout Acts (and really the whole New Testament), everything for the church flowed from and was built upon this central confession of Jesus as the Christ. All subsequent teaching, doctrine, and professed truth is tied to it and relies on it. It is fitting that the foundational truth

---

[7] This statement does not dismiss our individual responsibility; rather, it is intended to emphasize the communal nature of these images.

[8] G. K. Beale, *The Temple and the Church's Mission* (Downers Grove, IL: InterVarsity Press, 2004), 332.

collectively confirmed in the hearts and minds of the people of God as they gather is the truth about he who is truth: Jesus (John 14:6). When we gather as members of a local church, we are gathering around a central set of beliefs, a central and unified confession that defines us. It is not our gathering that defines us, but our belief. And it is this central confession of Christ as Savior and Lord that becomes the central focus around which all elements of the church are to be developed and taught. It is the central focus that determines the "why" and the "what" of the church's existence.

This confession serves as an anchor, a compass, and a filter. As an anchor, this confession grounds us in the essentials. It keeps us from being distracted by secondary and tertiary issues. It hones our focus to what is most important. As a compass, this confession points us to the pivotal. It keeps us heading in the right direction. It points our sight toward that from which we must not look away. As a filter, this confession pulls out the unhelpful. It keeps our message pure. It shows us what is beneficial and what is not. Our confession that Jesus is the Christ is the central focus that defines the true Christian church.

Do not miss this point. The confession of the church defines the church. Without this confession being biblically delineated regarding the person and work of Jesus, we end up more like members of a country club centered around our consumeristic preferences, creating gods and bibles in our own image. Whether intentionally or unintentionally, we end up worshiping ourselves instead of worshiping Jesus. Instead of engaging the culture, we capitulate to it. Instead of making disciples of Jesus, we end up making disciples of ourselves. We focus on what we think and feel is important without proper consideration of the biblical imperatives concerning who Jesus is, what he has done, and who we are to be in light of those truths. We end up without the biblically designed anchor, compass, and filter.

Unfortunately, I (Adam) have seen this happen many times in many ways. Years ago, I was attending a leadership conference at a large church near Louisville, Kentucky, with a friend of mine. My friend was the manager of a Christian radio station. He had recently begun attending a church, and he was struggling with the decision. He found the church he was attending was not clear regarding its position on baptism. Specifically, as he talked to other people in the church, he found that everyone had their own view regarding the purpose of baptism, whether it was essential, whether it saved you, whether you could be baptized without claiming faith in Jesus, and so on. No one with whom he spoke saw the lack of clarity as a big deal, so I encouraged him to ask someone on staff to clarify their beliefs due to the significance of baptism in the Bible as it relates to being a disciple of Jesus. He asked me to go with him to help him wade through any theological verbiage or implications. We approached a number of staff members, and over the course of the conversations, it became evident why people were unable to provide a clear answer to my friend's question. Their official position was personal preference, not biblical truth. Here's a summary of one of the conversations.

I asked, "Could you help answer some questions? My friend goes to church here, but is a little confused on your approach to baptism. He was wondering what the church's teaching on baptism is."

Someone responded, "Oh, we don't really focus on stuff like that."

"You don't really focus on stuff like what?" I questioned.

"We don't really focus on doctrine."

"Okay," I said, deciding to be a little more direct, "what does this church believe about baptism? Is baptism a necessary requirement for salvation, or is it an important symbol of salvation, but not a requirement?"

"Uh . . . well, see, different people on staff believe different things about that."

I pressed further. "Do you have a 'confession of faith' or 'statement of faith' that you put on the website or have posted somewhere that we could read regarding the central beliefs of this church?"

They almost laughed and looked at me sympathetically, as if I were a young child who just didn't know better. "No, that stuff just isn't important here. We just focus on worshiping God, and grace."

What could be more important than what is central in determining how to be made right with God and what determines where you spend eternity? There is a huge difference between simply trying to focus on the major issues and the response displayed by these staff members. They flippantly disregarded essential issues to which the Word of God directly speaks. We were asking about a salvation issue, about where someone spends eternity. We were asking about what makes someone a Christian. Whether or not baptism is required for salvation is an important question.[9] This church had about 6,000 people who attended every weekend, yet something was seriously wrong. The staff valued numbers and ensuring everyone was emotionally comfortable over clarity and truth.

The question is, What God are we worshiping? If a church is worshiping the God of the Bible, then the entirety of God's self-revelation determines

---

[9]   While baptism is incredibly important, the New Testament demonstrates that baptism is a public sign of the forgiveness of sins found through faith in Jesus Christ. See the discussion on pages 21–22.

who he is in our minds. Notice the staff member's emphasis on grace. Always focusing on only one aspect of God's character or attributes (in this case grace) while ignoring all others (such as justice) is not the worship of the one true God; it is the worship of an idol fashioned into what we want God to be. Another concern is, who determines what grace is and how it is applied? It seemed in this church, the listener makes that determination, and not any outside source or authority. The consumer decides. This is not worshiping Jesus the Christ, who is "the way, and the truth, and the life" (John 14:6). This is erecting a god made in our own image, just like the golden calf at the bottom of Mount Sinai (Exodus 32). While this church would publicly say that they believe Jesus is Lord, in reality, everything they did and planned to do was geared toward getting people in the building and making them feel comfortable. The church was not collectively seeking what Jesus wanted. They were not corporately acknowledging and surrendering to him as the Messiah. Their real confession was this: self is supreme.

Consumer-Centered or Christ-Centered Confession?

This perspective is nowhere near that of the early church, where the whole body and each individual member "devoted themselves to the apostles' teaching" (Acts 2:42). And what was it that the apostles were teaching? If we back up to the beginning of Acts, we find the answer. In chapter 1, Luke described Jesus's ascension into heaven and his last command to his followers. Jesus's followers were ready for him to establish his kingdom. They questioned, "Lord, will you at this time restore the kingdom to Israel?" (v. 6). They wanted to know when the kingdom would come, but Jesus was not interested in answering that question. Instead of focusing on when the kingdom would come in its fullness, Jesus focused them on their work, which was filling the kingdom. "It is not for you to know times or seasons that the Father has fixed by his own authority," he said. "But you will receive power when the Holy Spirit has come upon you, and *you will be my witnesses* in Jerusalem and in all Judea and Samaria, and to the end of the earth" (Acts 1:7–8). These early followers of Jesus were told that the Spirit would empower them to be his witnesses. Being a witness for Jesus meant they would serve Jesus's purposes, but it also meant that they would testify to others concerning who Jesus is: the Messiah. The use of the word "witnesses" shows that Jesus expected his followers to confess his person and work to others.

In the next chapter in Acts, at the first public gathering of people with the apostles, we see Peter standing up and teaching from the Old Testament that Jesus is the messianic Lord who saves all who believe in him (Acts 2:14–40). Throughout his sermon, he gave personal testimony of the nature of Jesus's death and resurrection and challenged everyone present to "repent and be baptized . . . in the name of Jesus Christ for the forgiveness of your sins" (Acts 2:38). The early church continually feasted on this truth regarding the person and work of Jesus. It was at the heart of all they did, and they devoted themselves to the reality that Jesus is the Christ.

The confession that Jesus is the Christ is the constant refrain of Scripture. Instead of "self-as-Lord," Scripture screams, "Jesus is Lord." We see this tradition of confession continuing in what Paul wrote to Timothy:

Great indeed, we confess, is the mystery of godliness:

> [Jesus] was manifested in the flesh,
>   vindicated by the Spirit,
>   seen by angels,
>   proclaimed among the nations,
>   believed on in the world,
>   taken up in glory. (1 Tim 3:16)

This verse is a shorthand confession of who Jesus is and what he has done. In fact, this verse is believed to be part of an early church hymn.[10] Early Christians used this shorthand confession of Jesus to worship and to share with others about him. This confession defined their life, worship, and evangelism.

The confession of Jesus as Lord is central. Paul, in the midst of his discussion on the place of Jews in the plan of God, explained why.

For Moses writes about the righteousness that is based on the law: that the person who does the commandments shall live by them. But the righteousness based on faith says, "Do not say in your heart, 'Who will ascend into heaven?'" (that is, to bring Christ down) "or 'Who will descend into the abyss?'" (that is, to bring Christ up from the dead). But what does it say? "The word is near you, in your mouth and in your heart" (that is, the word of faith that we proclaim); because, if you

---

[10]   Thomas D. Lea and Hayne P. Griffin Jr., *1, 2 Timothy and Titus*, New American Commentary 34 (Nashville: B&H, 1992), 124.

confess with your mouth that Jesus is Lord and believe in your heart that God raised him from the dead, you will be saved. For with the heart one believes and is justified, and with the mouth one confesses and is saved. For the Scripture says, "Everyone who believes in him will not be put to shame." For there is no distinction between Jew and Greek; for the same Lord is Lord of all, bestowing his riches on all who call on him. For "everyone who calls on the name of the Lord will be saved." (Rom 10:5–13)

Paul is here starkly contrasting "righteousness that is based on the law" with "righteousness based on faith." Where righteousness based on the law is concerned primarily with doing the commandments and living by them, righteousness based on faith is concerned primarily with the word of faith we proclaim. In other words, confessing who Jesus is and how his work affects who we are is the way we exercise faith. This passage reveals that to be "saved" is to confess him with your mouth and to believe in him in your heart. Paul pointed to the reality that it is through this confession one experiences salvation: whether Jew or Gentile. Salvation comes through faith in Jesus, exercised in verbal confession and belief. Thus, once more, Jesus, not self, is Lord. The way to life in Jesus is loving, trusting, believing in, and confessing him.

In his book *Desiring the Kingdom*, James K. A. Smith discusses how all cultural institutions (even secular ones, such as the mall, the stadium, and the academy) seek to form their participants in certain ways. The first major exercise in the book is to show that secular institutions are, in fact, centers of formation that target the heart and not the mind. One of Smith's most poignant examples is a shopping mall. The mall wants to form each consumer to be a certain kind of person: one that desires the products it sells. Smith then described the purchasing of items at a register as the "consummation of our worship." A "priest" invites us to give and to take, to taste and see with something concrete that the promises of the good life are true. We "make our sacrifice, leave our donation, but in return receive something with solidity that is wrapped in the colors and symbols of the saints and the season."[11] The reason Smith discussed the mall in such religious and ritual terms is to show that as an institution it is forming our hearts to love a certain vision of the good life. He continued:

---

[11]　James K. A. Smith, *Desiring the Kingdom: Worship, Worldview, and Cultural Formation* (Grand Rapids: Baker Academic, 2009), 22.

Because our hearts are oriented primarily by desire, by what we love, and because those desires are shaped and molded by the habit-forming practices in which we participate, it is the rituals and practices of the mall—the liturgies of mall and market—that shape our imaginations and how we orient ourselves to the world. Embedded in them is a common set of assumptions about the shape of human flourishing, which becomes an implicit *telos*, or goal, of our own desires and actions. That is, the visions of the good life embedded in these practices become surreptitiously embedded in us through our participation in the rituals and rhythms of these institutions.[12]

Once again, the real confession of the liturgy of the mall is "Self is supreme." Throughout his book, Smith asserts that our churches need to be centers of counter-formation, shaping participants into the kind of people who love Jesus and desire his kingdom. We need to be involved in individual and corporate liturgy,[13] holding fast to what the biblically defined church is and does. By doing this, our churches can effectively undo the formation toward consumerism and reform our desires toward loving Jesus as the Christ and his vision of the good life (see John 10:10).

After all, the way to life in Jesus is not knowing more; it is desiring, loving, and trusting him. However, without a central confession, we are left with a million self-confessions that are based on our preferences and cultural values and not on God. More often than not, the church has imported cultural values and strategies from the world (such as consumerism from the mall, nationalism from the stadium, or rationalism from the university) and baptized them.[14] This worldly approach does not lead to the glorification of King Jesus, but ultimately only of oneself.

Where Does This Confession Start?

I (Adam) have taught for years at a Christian university. Some of my classes are online. A few years ago, I was grading some discussion board posts. Discussion

---

[12]   Smith, *Desiring the Kingdom*, 25.

[13]   Do not be thrown off by this strange-sounding "High Church" word. Think: worship. *Liturgy* simply refers to "the physical acts of public worship." Smith's *Desiring the Kingdom* is the first in a series titled Cultural Liturgies, so this kind of language is built into Smith's argument.

[14]   This project of identifying and connecting various cultural values with their quintessential cultural institutions is also from Smith. See in particular chapter 3.

boards allow online students to interact with one another by providing feed-back on each other's ideas to produce community, accountability, and collaboration. One student was discussing a recent experience had at a church service. The student wrote, "The pastor preached about repentance, and I didn't like it. What about grace?" Do not miss the subjectivity. Did you notice that this student's starting point for truth was self-preference? What about the Bible? What about how God has chosen to reveal himself through his Son and in his Word? Repentance is an essential part of our relationship with God (Acts 20:21). This student was choosing to define God and how God acts toward us by how the student wanted him to be, not by how God has revealed himself.

Think about this: If you and I were walking down the street, came upon a random person, and I asked you to introduce him to me, you would look at me as if I were crazy. You could not introduce us, and I would have no basis for that expectation. Why? Because you do not know that person. You could make something up. You could develop an elaborate backstory, but it would be false. To accurately describe someone, one first has to get information from that individual, the source. You have to know him to describe him. Even if someone else tells you about a person, you need to confirm it with the person himself to make sure it is true. In the same way, for us to be confident in who God is, we need his self-description. Let me be clear: we are not in the dark concerning who God is and what he ultimately desires. He has revealed himself to us. He has given us a wealth of information about how he works. He has revealed himself in Jesus, given us the Bible, and even given us his Spirit. We have received this information from him, and thus we can know him.

What we are to have as central in our confession and what we are to rally our lives around is not self; it is the identity of Jesus as Christ the Messiah. This truth is revealed time and time again in the Scriptures. The central confession of our lives is that Jesus is the Son of God, who came and lived, died, and rose again, fulfilling the requirements of the law on our behalf and providing us with forgiveness of all our sin. In his time, he will return to judge all of humanity and to separate his own, forgiven children from those who are not forgiven. For us to receive forgiveness of sins, we need to repent of our sins, believe this good news, and make it the central confession of our lives and our corporate gatherings.

At this point, you may be asking, "How does the church confess Jesus? How does it communicate that Jesus is the Messiah and Lord? Are we saying that to confess is simply to say that Jesus is Lord? Are we saying that the church congregation must verbalize together that the Messiah has come?"

Not exactly, though those things are surely good and right to do. There are three primary ways that the church historically and biblically has revealed Jesus as Lord: through the preaching of the Word of God, through water baptism, and through the Lord's Supper. By these three avenues, Jesus is proclaimed in biblical, gospel-believing churches. They collectively show who Jesus is to the watching world, but much more importantly and centrally, it is through these avenues that we as a body affirm the truth and remind one another of the central truths of Jesus's identity.

Surely the clearest of the three, in biblical preaching the truth of the identity of Jesus is proclaimed. The text of Scripture points to Jesus on every page, if not in word, then certainly in idea and end goal. Timothy Keller has said, "Every time you expound a Bible text, you are not finished unless you demonstrate how it shows us that we cannot save ourselves and that only Jesus can."[15] This is the point and goal of preaching: to confess Christ as Lord. Keller goes on to say, "This is how to deliver not just an informative lecture but a life-changing sermon. It is not merely to talk about Christ but to show him, to 'demonstrate' [see 1 Cor 2:4] his greatness and to reveal him as worthy of praise and adoration."[16]

Confession (like preaching) is more than speaking of Christ (though it is not less), and the other two primary ways that the church confesses Jesus is Lord are much more about showing. In fact, both baptism and the Lord's Supper are acts performed by the members of the church to show and remind one another of who Jesus is and what he has done. Baptism, in particular, is a "show-and-tell" situation. First, when the candidate is asked, "What is your confession of faith?" (in other words, "Who is Jesus to you?"), the expected response is that Jesus is the person's Lord and Savior, the Messiah of the whole world, and that it is in him and him alone that the candidate is trusting for salvation. This verbal confession is made publicly and purposefully. This public confession (alongside good works) is to serve as evidence of conversion. It is then followed by a physical act, a bodily confession, if you will. The person is lowered into the water, which symbolizes the reality of our spiritual death before being cleansed by Jesus. He or she is then raised up and out of the water as a symbol of resurrection and new life. The act of baptism proclaims that Jesus is the Messiah, the one who is making all things—in this case the person's individual life—new. This is the example set by the early church:

[15] Timothy Keller, *Preaching: Communicating Faith in an Age of Skepticism* (London: Penguin Books, 2016), 48.
[16] Keller, 17–18.

But when they believed Philip as he proclaimed the good news of the kingdom of God and the name of Jesus Christ, they were baptized, both men and women. (Acts 8:12)

Crispus, the synagogue leader, and his entire household believed in the Lord; and many of the Corinthians who heard Paul believed and were baptized. (Acts 18:8)[17]

Finally, the ordinance of the Lord's Supper is also an avenue of confession for the church. The origin of the Lord's Supper is recorded in Matthew 26. This passage recounts the scene as Jesus shared the Passover meal with his disciples right before he was to be betrayed and crucified: "Now as they were eating, Jesus took bread, and after blessing it broke it and gave it to the disciples, and said, 'Take, eat; this is my body.' And he took a cup, and when he had given thanks he gave it to them, saying, 'Drink of it, all of you, for this is my blood of the covenant, which is poured out for many for the forgiveness of sins'" (vv. 26–28). Here Jesus adds to the traditional Passover meal. He expects that his Jewish followers will continue to observe Passover, and he tells them to remember his death, as their King and Messiah, for their sins at this moment in the Passover meal. The majority of those reading this book are probably not Jewish and, thus, do not observe Passover; however, Christian churches continue this tradition that Jesus began of remembering his death with bread and wine. Looking back, we proclaim to one another with a meal that Jesus died for our sins, that his body was broken and his blood spilled. We further proclaim that Jesus is the Messiah and look forward to the day when we will share a meal together with the global church, celebrating the final consummation of the kingdom of God.

Many Churches, One Confession

There are many differing Christian denominations in our modern context. From Baptist and Presbyterian to Wesleyan and Charismatic/Pentecostal

---

[17] See also Acts 8:36–38; 10:47–48; 16:14–15; 16:31–33. Some argue that infants would have been a part of some of these "household" baptisms. That argument from silence is used as a justification for infant baptism without a confession of faith; however, that is an assumption. Nowhere in the text are infants mentioned, and the consistent pattern throughout the Gospels and Acts is that someone responds positively to the good news about Jesus and then is baptized. Thus, we are advocating for a "believer's" baptism, since that seems to be the model set for us by the early church.

churches, many differences exist when it comes to church government, leadership structure, evangelistic zeal, discipleship practices, worship liturgy, Communion, sanctification, the order of salvation, and free will. In the midst of all these differences, what makes any gathering, regardless of the denomination (or lack thereof), a Christian church? Is it meeting together? Is it shared worship of the King? Partly, but foundationally, the central element that marks a Christian church gathering is its confession of Jesus as Lord.

What we confess as *a church* determines whether or not we are a part of *the church*, that is, the global or universal church. Let us step back for a moment and flesh this out a little more.

In the original language of the New Testament, Greek, the word from which we get our English word *church* is *ekklesia* (ἐκκλησία). This Greek word was not originally a religious term; typically, it referred to a purposefully gathered assembly of people. The New Testament Christians appropriated this political word for their own gatherings because they too were purposefully gathering as a people.

There seem to be two basic ways this word is used in the Bible. It is used of both a local gathering of Christians and the total collection of all Christians. This is why we can speak of *the church* and *a church* and mean different things. A representative example of the local use of *ekklesia* is found in Acts 8:1: "And there arose on that day a great persecution against the church in Jerusalem, and they were all scattered throughout the regions of Judea and Samaria, except the apostles." This passage describes a situation in the life of a local church in a single city. On the other hand, a representative example of the global use of *ekklesia* is found in Matt 16:18: "And I tell you, you are Peter, and on this rock I will build my church, and the gates of hell shall not prevail against it." Here Jesus is saying that he will build his church on Peter's confession of him as Lord. This is a reference not to a particular congregation, but to all those who will be a part of the body of Christ.

The chapters of this book refer primarily to characteristics of local churches. Our local churches are to be confessing, gathering, praying, giving, and engaging bodies. While it is true that the universal church should be a praying, giving, and engaging church, the universal church is not, as a whole, a gathering church. Local congregations are the way the church gathers.

Another way to think about it is like this: A *local* church is a congregation that gathers together, confesses Jesus as Lord (through preaching, baptism, and the Lord's Supper), prays, engages, and gives wherever that body is in the world. All local churches are committed to the same mission: preaching the gospel and confessing Jesus. All of these local churches all over the world, united by gospel mission and discipleship, then make up the *global* church. There can be a distinct difference between saying one is part of *the* church and saying one belongs to *a* church. Notice how this has been defined lest there be any misunderstanding: one cannot be recognized as a member of *the* church unless one is a part of a local church. Why? The sum total of the local churches, or congregations, in the kingdom of God make up the church global. That does not necessarily mean that if someone is not a member of a local church, he or she is not saved. Rather, these statements reflect the reality that throughout the history of the church, and as evidenced in Acts, one was identified with the church of Jesus by being an active part of a local church. Make no mistake: there are many expressions of the local church, from the modern, Western megachurch to the house church, but the universal church of God is a community experience, whatever that community looks like. What we confess as a local church about Jesus our Lord determines whether or not we are a part of the global church.

Central to this confession is that Jesus is the Christ, the Messiah. Our confession of faith in Jesus is that which we hold forth for all to see, that which we unite around, and that which we proclaim centrally in all that we do! The apostle Paul proclaimed in Romans 10, "If you confess with your mouth that Jesus is Lord and believe in your heart that God raised him from the dead, you will be saved. For with the heart one believes and is justified, and with the mouth one confesses and is saved" (vv. 9–10). This confession is essential for salvation, should be central to our lives, and must be central to our worship.

Many of today's "Christian" churches seem to have an awful lot of confessions that have very little to do with Christ as Lord. When we are honest, in any church where Jesus as the Christ is not the central confession, what is put on their signs, the slogans slapped on their websites, the songs that are sung, the "pop psychology" that is preached, and the programming that is provided is all unintentionally geared to promote the worship, not of King Jesus, but of self.

Let us pause and reflect. We must be careful not to assume too much, but to genuinely question ourselves and our worship gatherings. Are we defined by an unapologetic, age-old pronouncement that Jesus is the Savior of the world? Are our church gatherings? Are we defined by a gospel of self or the gospel of King Jesus?

Just as I (Adam) am still defined by my confession to Adrienne when I was eighteen that I loved her and wanted her to be my wife, so too our churches individually and corporately must be defined by the confession that we love Jesus, and that he is our Lord and Savior. Just as the confession of my love for my future wife came over time and grew in depth, so too should our confession of Christ. It should grow and not be stagnant. It is not a onetime confession, but a persistent conviction. Just as my confession to Adrienne was a confession not only of words, but of practices, so too our confession of Jesus should be transformative for our lives. My confession to Adrienne was the root that fed what I did in our relationship. So too must our love for Christ. My prayer for you is that you are realizing a new depth to this confession today. May our confession provide the lifeblood for all that we do.

Final Thoughts

How would our approach to "church" be different if this confession of Jesus as Lord drove our thoughts and actions? For anyone currently looking for a church, this confession should be your preeminent consideration regarding a church. A gospel-centric confession must be the number-one priority when joining the membership of a local body of believers. One should determine if this local church publicly cherishes and confesses Christ as central to all it does, not merely as a creative slogan or mission statement, but as the true foundation and only solid rock. Remember the avenues of confession we discussed, and find a church that values biblical preaching, baptism, and the Lord's Supper not for their own sake, but as ways to point to Jesus.[18] Resist the urge to look for a church to meet your consumeristic needs and programming styles, but search diligently to find a church that makes much of Jesus. Find one in which you can contribute to the body with the gifts that Jesus has given you by means of the indwelling work of his Spirit (see Rom 12:3–21; 1 Cor 12:1–31; Eph 4:1–16). We as the body of Christ are called to unite around the confession that Jesus is the Messiah just as the early church did. It should be the center of our preaching and teaching. It should direct our conversations and encouragement. It should drive our passion for the church to confess and worship anew the risen Christ when we meet together. It should shape our lives during the week.

Ask yourself, "What is my central confession? What do I believe wholeheartedly?" Is central in your confession of faith the conviction that Jesus is the Christ, the Messiah? Do you believe that this Christ, the Son of God, came to earth and lived, died, and rose again, fulfilling the requirements of

---

[18] If you think that you need a little more help with what to look for in a church, keep reading! There are more characteristics to be discussed. We would also encourage you to check out Mark Dever, *Nine Marks of a Healthy Church* (Wheaton, IL: Crossway, 2013).

the law on our behalf and providing us with forgiveness from all our sin? Maybe you realize today that this *is* your confession, and you are willing to submit every aspect of your life to Jesus Christ. Or maybe there is one aspect of life that you have been withholding from his will. Confess today and turn that over to him. Maybe you suddenly realize the need to take seriously all the teachings of Christ, and you recognize that you have never made a confession publicly and been baptized as a believer. I encourage you to contact your pastor and move forward with this next phase of spiritual life. If you are not a member of a church, I want to encourage you to join a healthy, Bible-believing, Christ-exalting church such as we discussed a moment ago.

Maybe you are firmer in your belief today than you have ever been. If so, stand firm in that confession and ask God to root you deeply in it and not allow anything this world throws at you to move you. Ask him to give you more confidence in Christ and more joy in him than you have ever had.

Let us commit to follow the example of the early church. Just as the confession that Jesus is the Christ served as central to all they did and believed, may it be the same for us, both individually as believers and corporately as a church. May we, together with the apostle Paul, confess:

Great indeed . . . is the mystery of godliness:

> [Jesus] was manifested in the flesh,
>   vindicated by the Spirit,
>   seen by angels,
>   proclaimed among the nations,
>   believed on in the world,
>   taken up in glory. (1 Tim 3:16)

Personal Reflection or
Group Discussion Questions

1. Before reading this chapter, would you have been able to define the confession of the church? If not, what would your definition have been and how has a greater understanding of the biblical confession of the church already shifted your answer?

2. Have you ever felt alone or without community? If so, how is the gospel of who Jesus is and what he has done good news to the lonely or marginalized? And how is this good news to you at this moment?

3. Do you confess the Messiah Jesus as Lord? If not, what fear or doubt is holding you back? If so, is there still some element of your life that you are reluctant to submit completely to Jesus's reign? Are you willing to take the next step and surrender that thing to Jesus's will today?

4. How involved are you in your local church? What does this show about your priorities? What in your current cultural setting is forming your love and desire for things other than God? Are you engaged in corporate practices that can reorient your heart toward God? Are you engaged in individual disciplines that can reorient your heart toward God? Do you spend enough time in community with other believers to counter the formation of the worldly culture?

5. Is your confession of Jesus defined by God's self-revelation in Scripture? When you think of who Jesus is, does your mind go to passages of the Bible? If not, what does define your understanding of Jesus? How can you effectively change your mental image of Jesus to be more biblical?

6. How do you currently invite others to your local church? How do you describe it to them? What do you focus on? Are you more concerned with the quality of the teaching and corporate confessions or more excited about the programs and the popularity of the preacher?

Devotional

Day One: Acts 10:34–43

Have you ever been hesitant to confess something you believe or know to be true?

Open your Bible and read Acts 10:34–43.

In this passage, Peter confesses what he knows to be true about Jesus. This confession put him at odds with the Jewish leaders and much of the Jewish people.

Think deeply about the following questions:

What stands out to you about Peter's confession? What elements are featured prominently in it?

Why is it significant that he points out that we have been commanded to preach and to testify about who Jesus is?

How did Peter have the courage to proclaim and confess with boldness that Jesus is the Christ? Do you have this same courage? If not, what is holding you back from this type of radical obedience?

Reflect on the fact that you too can be empowered by the Holy Spirit to confess that Jesus is Messiah and Lord, even in a crowd like the one Peter addressed. What does it mean that you can also be empowered by the Holy Spirit to make this confession? What might that look like?

How can you prepare to confess Jesus as Lord this week? What does this look like in your workplace? At home? With friends?

Devotional

Day Two: Acts 2:22–36

Have you ever been given an opportunity to confess who Jesus is to friends, coworkers, or family members? How did you handle it?

Open your Bible and read Acts 2:22–36.

In this passage, God gives Peter the opportunity to share with thousands of people concerning who Jesus was and is. Through the leading of the Holy Spirit, Peter does so powerfully.

Think deeply about the following questions:

In the past, have you responded as Peter did in being obedient to the leading of the Holy Spirit? What fears do you still need to overcome? What biblical truth and promise of God and his kingdom do you need to reflect on to be motivated to share a similar confession with those who need to hear?

Reflect on the significance of Pentecost and Peter proclaiming the Messiah at that particular time.

What elements are featured prominently in Peter's confession? What similar elements should be present in our confessions?

Why does Peter quote from Ps 16:8–11? What is the significance of that passage? It may be helpful to read Psalm 16 and consider how its context relates to the biblical-theological context of Acts 2.

What can you be doing to prepare for the moments God will give you to confess Jesus as Lord and Messiah to those who need to hear? Are you committing Scripture to memory and praying for opportunities to share the good news with others?

Devotional

Day Three: Acts 3:11–26

Have you ever been confronted by someone about a mistake you made? Have you ever had to confront someone else about something?

Open your Bible and read Acts 3:11–26.

In this passage, Peter loudly confronts the Jewish people for crucifying their King, then preaches the gospel to them.

Think deeply about the following questions:

Why is the confession in this passage a controversial one?

In what ways are you and I like the Jewish leaders whom Peter addressed?

There is not just condemnation in the confession in this passage, but also good news. What is the good news?

How will God's people be turned from their wickedness? Why is this good news for us today?

How might this confession of the gospel of Jesus Christ motivate us to obedience this week?

Devotional

Day Four: Romans 10:5–13

In what are you trusting for salvation? Does your performance today give you self-worth? Are you relying on your goodness for salvation?

Open your Bible and read Romans 10:5–13.

Think deeply about the following questions:

Do good works provide salvation or worthiness before God? What does this passage say brings salvation? What must one do to be saved?

In this passage, why is confession tied to belief?

Have you ever truly confessed with your mouth and believed in your heart that Jesus is the risen Lord?

The life of faith is not one only for individuals; it is radically community oriented. How does the church gathering play into this discussion of confession?

Why does physically confessing the truth about Jesus have spiritual significance?

How can you more intentionally confess Christ this week as an individual and as a member of a church body? How can you practically serve others to put this confession on display for others this week?

Devotional

Day Five: Isaiah 53:7–12

Have you ever faced verbal or physical persecution or any other form of physical violence?

Open your Bible and read Isaiah 53:7–12.

In this passage, the prophet Isaiah prophesied that the Messiah will bear the iniquities and transgressions of God's people by suffering and dying on their behalf.

Think deeply about the following questions:

Why is understanding Jesus as the Suffering Servant of Isaiah's prophecy an important part of the Christian confession of who Jesus is?

What is the significance of Isaiah's reference to a lamb being "led to the slaughter"?

Why was this idea of a man suffering on behalf of others revolutionary in the ancient Near East?

Why is this idea surprising to a modern audience? Why is this idea good news for you today?

CHAPTER 2

GATHERING CHURCH:
We Live in Community

Gathering both formally and informally was a central characteristic of the early church as detailed in the book of Acts.

> And they *devoted themselves to* the apostles' teaching and *the fellowship, to the breaking of bread* and the prayers. And awe came upon every soul, and many wonders and signs were being done through the apostles. And all who believed were together and had all things in common. And they were selling their possessions and belongings and distributing the proceeds to all, as any had need. *And day by day,* attending the temple *together* and *breaking bread in their homes,* they received their food with glad and generous hearts, praising God and having favor with all the people. And the Lord added to their number day by day those who were being saved. (Acts 2:42–47)

In high school, there was a particular group of friends with whom I (Jared) always enjoyed hanging out. One of our regular gathering places was the lunchroom table, where we met primarily not to eat but to play cards. Whether we were playing Hearts, President, or Liar, we always had a great time and thoroughly enjoyed one another's company. We were friends, and though each wanted to win whatever game we happened to be playing, we cared about one another. We would go to bat for one another. We connected with and encouraged one another. Sure, we got mad every once in a while, but we always calmed down. Gathering together was immensely important to us, but not in and of itself. Our gathering was important because it facilitated the other things we did. Our gathering allowed for card playing, laughter, meal sharing, and political and philosophical discussion. In fact, foundationally, it facilitated our friendship.

Similarly, a fundamental characteristic of the church is that it gathers regularly and faithfully, as demonstrated throughout Acts and the Epistles of the New Testament. The original meaning for the word *church* involved a gathering (an assembly) of people. While the word itself should be sufficient to demonstrate the necessity for the people of God to gather regularly, God graciously gave us example after example throughout the New Testament not only to describe the early church's activity but also to serve as a model for believers so we could know and follow God's design for us today. Members of the body of Christ are called to spend time together. This gathering time should be corporate and continual. As evidenced in Acts 2:42–47 and elsewhere, the gathering of the church is essential in part because it is through these gatherings that the primary mission of the church is facilitated. A church gathers together to help make disciples: to bring the lost to Christ while maturing saints in Christ (Matt 28:19–20).[1] A church that gathers only for the sake of gathering is unhealthy and may soon no longer be a church at all. The goal of this chapter is to explain one aspect of what the meeting of the church on the Lord's Day is for and how the church keeps that commitment to community even after Sunday becomes Monday and the rest of the week.

Two Modes of Gathering

The early church was devoted to "the fellowship" (Acts 2:42). This fellowship was more than just being present together; this declaration of fellowship in

---

[1]   Matthew 28:19–20 uniquely highlights the purpose of the church members to go and make disciples by baptizing them (bringing people to Jesus) and teaching them (maturing them in Jesus). Both evangelism and maturation are part of discipleship. That being said, it seems throughout the New Testament that the primary purpose of the gathering time corporately was to equip believers to go out and do ministry in the world (Eph 4:11–14), while the church individually was sent out from those gathering times to win people to Jesus (Matt 28:19–20; notice the call to "go" and "make"; while the command is to make disciples, this command is carried out by the church as they are going). While Paul expected unbelievers to be present during church gatherings, as evidenced by the "outsider" language in 1 Cor 14:16, the primary focus of the church gathering was for the maturing and training of the saints in the work and will of God.

connection with the rest of the verse reveals that the early church intentionally experienced a meaningful, close relationship resembling a family.[2] This family gathered to grow in their understanding of their Messiah Jesus (apostles' teaching), to eat together, and to pray together (Acts 2:42).[3] Throughout Acts, we find that while the early church had established formal gatherings, they also regularly experienced life together in less formal gatherings throughout their weeks. This model is instructive for us.

The church is called to gather together in two distinct modes: corporately and continually. The church gathers together in a large group setting to worship the Lord Jesus collectively and to proclaim the gospel and its implications to one another. This is the corporate gathering. In this time, the members' hearts are reoriented away from various "loves" fostered by the world and once more back to their "first love," Christ the King (see Rev 2:4 NASB). This corporate gathering is a time for the equipping of the saints so that they might be better prepared to go and make disciples by reaching their world for Jesus and encouraging other believers along the way (Eph 4:11–16).

The church should also gather in smaller group settings throughout the week, in the midst of normal life.[4] This type of gathering will not include the entire local congregation, but will involve various members of that congregation as their lives intentionally intersect for kingdom purposes. While these situations are primarily for the discipleship of the body of Christ, this is also an excellent opportunity for our unbelieving friends and neighbors to see the kingdom of God breaking into the world. Invite them, in fact, and they will get a front row seat to Christian community in all its goodness and difficulty. Each of us is individually called to take the good news of King Jesus to the world. We are called to serve him and live for Jesus in the midst of the rhythm of life; however, we are not to do this alone, but as the church. When we intentionally connect with one another during the workweek, we foster community and hospitality, temptation is restrained, we remind one another of the gospel, and needs are met. Many local churches are good at organizing a corporate gathering that fosters genuine worship, but these churches can easily miss the importance of life-on-life discipleship that frequent, smaller, and

---

[2]   Hellerman, *When the Church Was a Family*, 130 (see chap. 1, n. 6). See also 1 Cor 1:9; 5:2 NIV; 1 John 1:3, 6–7.

[3]   John B. Polhill, *Acts: An Exegetical and Theological Exposition of Holy Scripture*, New American Commentary 26 (Nashville: B&H, 1992), 119.

[4]   This statement is not arguing for a "small group" ministry, but maintaining that in small, intimate groups, the early church was faithfully connecting and investing in one another's lives. Today, we as the present church should continue to meet as part of the family of God throughout our week. These "throughout the week" smaller gatherings are vital.

more intimate gatherings facilitate. Other churches focus heavily on small groups and can likewise miss the necessity of the entire body worshiping together in anticipation of God's coming kingdom. The goal is to gather both corporately and continually, as portrayed in the New Testament, so that the church is able to move forward with its mission of making disciples.

A Biblical Church Gathers Corporately

Let us talk more about the corporate gathering of God's people. A congregation typically gathers as "the church" each Sunday, but this same group of people does not cease to be the church when they leave the building.[5] Church does not end when Sunday morning is over. Sunday is a gathering time to prepare us as the church for our weekly engagements. Sunday morning is not when we *are at* church. Sunday prepares us *to be* the church: both when gathered and when scattered.[6] James K. A. Smith described how this works: "The church—the body of Christ—is . . . where God invites us to renew our loves, reorient our desires, and restrain our appetites . . . Christian worship is the feast where we acquire new hungers—for God and for what God desires—and are then sent into his creation to act accordingly."[7] When we gather corporately, we are to submit our desires to the Lord together and prepare to exit into the world with our love fixed solely on God. Our corporate gathering should prepare us to love God and people well throughout the week. Then, we should be regularly engaging one another in preparation for the next all-inclusive gathering, where we will again reorient our love toward God.[8] This approach outlines the system that God has set forth for our good. The corporate gathering prepares us to be the church. We go out together from the weekly worship service to be the church to the world before returning to prepare again. This God-given design is extremely helpful—essential, even.

Acts 20:7 is one of the many passages that point to the expectation of the

---

[5]   The building is not the church. The building is called a "church building," not because the building itself is special, but because it is in this place that the real church, the people of God, gather to worship.

[6]   By "scattered," I mean when we leave. Each believer is a part of the church, and each person's identity as part of the church (the body of Jesus) does not change when that person leaves the corporate gathering time.

[7]   James K. A. Smith, *You Are What You Love: The Spiritual Power of Habit* (Grand Rapids: Brazos, 2016), 65.

[8]   While Acts provides glimpses into this practice and intention in the corporate gathering, it is perhaps most clearly evidenced in the content and circumstances of the Epistles Paul wrote to various churches. Most of Paul's letters were to local congregations, providing instructions on how they should act when gathered and the fruit those instructions should bear on their lives from day to day.

corporate gathering. This narrative, penned by Luke, is not just descriptive of what the church did back then, but is a model for us to follow in principle today. It is instructive. Luke explained, "On the first day of the week, when we were gathered together to break bread, Paul talked with [those gathered], intending to depart on the next day, and he prolonged his speech until midnight." The first day of the week was their regular appointed gathering time in honor of the resurrected Lord, and this time was strategic for believers. From the very beginning of the church, the "Lord's Day" (Sunday, since that is when Jesus was resurrected) has been the Christian day of intentional gathering.[9] This does not mean that believers cannot have other days for gathering corporately. Due to the size of the gathering and other practical restrictions, such as work schedules, some people cannot meet on Sunday. While we believe it is instructive that they chose to meet on the day the Lord was resurrected, we also acknowledge the key principle communicated in this text: the church met weekly as a unified corporate body to worship God together.

As we look further at how the church met in Acts and the rest of the New Testament, we see that this weekly gathering time was used

- for fellowship and accountability (Acts 2:42–47; 1 Cor 6:1–8; Gal 6:1–2; Eph 4:25; Titus 2:1–8)
- to encourage one another in their walk with the Lord (Acts 2:42–47; 1 Cor 14:3, 12, 26; 1 Thess 5:11; Heb 10:24–25)
- to learn and grow through Scripture reading and teaching (Acts 2:42–47; 1 Tim 4:13; 2 Tim 4:1–2)
- to celebrate through song and prayer (Acts 2:42–47; 4:24; Eph 5:19–20; Col 3:16)

Regarding these first three, you cannot have genuine fellowship, accountability, and encouragement by passively watching a service on television or a computer monitor. God did not design a church gathering to be a place merely

---

[9]   Much debate exists on this verse. The first debate concerns whether the verse reveals that this *particular* meeting was on the first day of the week or if it reveals the historical pattern of the early church in meeting on the first day of each week. The second debate concerns whether the "first day of the week" began on Saturday night or on Sunday morning. If Luke was following a Jewish calendar, then the meeting was on Saturday night; however, if he following a Roman calendar, then the meeting was on Sunday. In whole, the strongest evidence points to this meeting being on Sunday and the Sunday meeting being a pattern for the church. See Darrell L. Bock, *Acts*, Baker Exegetical Commentary on the New Testament (Grand Rapids: Baker, 2007), 619–20; Eckhard J. Schnabel, *Acts*, Exegetical Commentary on the New Testament (Grand Rapids: Zondervan, 2012), 834–35; and David G. Peterson, *The Acts of the Apostles*, Pillar New Testament Commentary (Grand Rapids: Eerdmans, 2009), 557–58. This is against Steven Ger, *Acts: Witnesses to the World* (Chattanooga: AMG, 2004), eBook, 2006.

to receive; instead, he intended it to be a place of engagement, where each person would use his or her personality, gifts, and passions for the glory of God in meeting with the saints to publicly acknowledge Jesus as the Christ. There is nothing inherently wrong with watching services through these media. Doing so is helpful, but we cannot use them as a substitute for gathering with the church as the church.[10] The screen is no substitute for the church. Real people with real issues need your contribution to the body of Christ. We are self-serving when we do not gather with the body of believers and use our own gifting to edify and serve others. In fact, I (Adam) heard a local pastor talking about live streaming services and how this platform has helped some people feel connected to the church. As a result, tithes and offerings have gone up and stayed more consistent. The pastor went on to enthusiastically describe a time when one of his congregants posted on social media that they had decided to sleep in, and they were thankful that they could still "have church" through the internet. That is not church.

Church cannot be passively experienced, like a movie or a play. There is more to it than that. Hebrews 10 offers this counsel:

> Therefore, brothers, since we have confidence to enter the holy places by the blood of Jesus, by the new and living way that he opened for us through the curtain, that is, through his flesh, and since we have a great priest over the house of God, let us draw near with a true heart in full assurance of faith, with our hearts sprinkled clean from an evil conscience and our bodies washed with pure water. Let us hold fast the confession of our hope without wavering, for he who promised is faithful. And let us consider how to stir up one another to love and good works, not neglecting to meet together, as is the habit of some, but encouraging one another, and all the more as you see the Day drawing near. (vv. 19–25)

The author of Hebrews affirmed the confidence that we have in the work of Jesus. He is our great high priest, whose work on the cross was the sufficient sacrifice that dealt with sin. In light of our confidence in Christ's work, the author exhorted his readers to hold fast to the confession of who Jesus is and what he has done. He also exhorted them to continue to meet together

---

[10]   If the internet service has a unique engagement platform where attendees connect in a personal and authentic way with one another beyond merely passively observing a service, then this critique may not apply; however, such approaches to internet "church" are rare.

for the purpose of encouragement. The weekly meeting of believers together is tied to the confidence we have in Jesus and the encouragement we need. We cannot encourage others or engage in discipleship when we view a church service on TV or a computer screen. These meetings are thus so much more than hearing a sermon and singing songs (which can be done when passively viewing a screen), but they are an expression of faith in the coming Jesus, and they facilitate encouragement and discipleship.

Even celebrating Jesus through song is something that should be done in community. This does not mean that we should not celebrate through song privately. We should praise God privately, but we must also acknowledge that singing with the radio or a live-streamed service without other believers is missing out on the full design God has for that gathering moment. Paul wrote:

> And do not get drunk with wine, for that is debauchery, but be filled with the Spirit, *addressing one another in psalms and hymns and spiritual songs, singing and making melody to the Lord with your heart,* giving thanks always and for everything to God the Father in the name of our Lord Jesus Christ, submitting to one another out of reverence for Christ. (Eph 5:18–21)

A component of God's design for Spirit-filled worship is that the body would corporately make melodious declarations in the presence of one another as they collectively display and declare their affections for God. That is why, if you notice, many of our worship songs are collective prayers we sing together, affirming and encouraging one another in the faith.

Benefits of Gathering Corporately

Why does the church have physical, public worship, and why does it matter if we participate? Being together creates an environment conducive to encouragement, correction, and transformation in community. Smith said it this way: "If sanctification is tantamount to closing the gap between what I know and what I do, it means changing what I want. And that requires submitting ourselves to disciplines and regimens that reach down into our deepest habits."[11] All of us have the common experience of knowing what is right, but we end up doing the

---

[11] Smith, *You Are What You Love*, 65.

opposite, that which we know to be wrong. What we choose is what we truly desire, and our choices frequently show that we end up desiring what we know to be wrong. This is the common experience that Smith is speaking to: we desire the wrong things. He suggests that changing our desires requires submitting to "disciplines and regimens" that will ultimately affect our habits. Our desires are changed, for better or for worse, by the disciplines and liturgy we submit ourselves to (or allow ourselves to be submitted to). Corporate worship aids us here. The things we do as a body when we gather together as a church matter because they form us into the kind of people that love God and one another. The very acts of worship the church submits to shape us in ways that can affect our habits and affections. A few examples: bowing our heads and our hearts in prayer shapes us to be humble and contrite before our God and King. Singing corporately can shape us to desire the coming kingdom, where we will frequently sing the praises of our Savior. Corporate singing also reminds us that we are all equal before the throne (Eph 2:11–22). Tasting the drink and bread in Communion reminds us of the price that was paid for our salvation and pushes us to love the one who gave himself up for the sake of his bride (1 Cor 1:26; 2 Cor 5:14–15; Gal 2:20). Sitting under the teaching of the Word and submitting to church elders forms us to be the kind of people who submit to the head Shepherd, Jesus, and obey his words (Heb 13:17; 1 Pet 5:1–11). The church has physical, public worship because it forms us to be the kind of people that love Jesus, love his bride, and hope for the consummation of his kingdom.[12]

The times when the early church met were strategic and are also important for our consideration. Their times together were designed to encourage and equip believers to go and engage the world. The apostle Paul further explained this equipping:

> And he gave the apostles, the prophets, the evangelists, the shepherds and teachers, to equip the saints for the work of ministry, for building up the body of Christ, until we all attain to the unity of the faith and of the knowledge of the Son of God, to mature manhood, to

---

[12] This paragraph discusses only some examples of corporate liturgy and disciplines that form us to be people who love Jesus. There are also many disciplines for individuals (such as Bible study and reading, prayer, meditation, and fasting) that shape us spiritually. The focus of this chapter is simply on the corporate gathering. Any good disciplines that an individual submits to should be balanced by healthy corporate worship and integration as well (if at all possible). Even the most well-intentioned personal devotion can form us toward individualism and modern notions of autonomy without the church gathering as a helpful reminder of the true corporate nature of the church and opportunity for engagement in discipleship. For more, see Donald S. Whitney's books *Spiritual Disciplines within the Church: Participating Fully in the Body of Christ* (Chicago: Moody, 1996) and *Spiritual Disciplines for the Christian Life*, rev. ed. (Colorado Springs: NavPress, 2014).

the measure of the stature of the fullness of Christ, so that we may no longer be children, tossed to and fro by the waves and carried about by every wind of doctrine, by human cunning, by craftiness in deceitful schemes. Rather, speaking the truth in love, we are to grow up in every way into him who is the head, into Christ, from whom the whole body, joined and held together by every joint with which it is equipped, when each part is working properly, makes the body grow so that it builds itself up in love. (Eph 4:11–16)

The church gathering is principally an in-house affair, so to speak. The point of the gathering is for various believers with various spiritual gifts to work together to equip the saints for the work of ministry. We are all to use our gifting to edify, encourage, and build up the body of Christ so that we all mature, grow, and attain the unity of the faith. That is the vision of the church the New Testament casts.

This vision cannot be accomplished across an impersonal media platform. The New Testament vision of the church is a very personal one. It assumes church members know one another and are invested in each other's lives. The individualism of the modern West conditions us to think in terms of only what benefits me. How does this church fit my needs? How does it contribute to my spiritual growth? While these are sometimes legitimate questions to ask of a church, the central, driving attitude in the hearts and minds of believers involved in the local church should be one of self-giving and service of others. How can I use my gifts to edify the body? How can I serve my fellow believers? Peter described Christians as "living stones" who are "being built up as a spiritual house" (1 Pet 2:5). This dramatic metaphor for the church shows how connected and dependent we should be concerning our fellow church members. We are only the church together, and we are only truly together when we regularly meet together.

While the primary purpose of the corporate church gathering is for the edifying and discipling of the believer, this does not mean that unsaved people are not invited. They were present in the early church gatherings and should be present in ours. The church gathering was designed so that in the midst of the worship and discipleship of the believer, the lost person might see believers exalting the risen Savior, be convicted of their sin, and choose to believe in Jesus, as 1 Corinthians 14 makes evident.[13]

---

[13]   In 1 Corinthians 14, Paul describes a situation that may occur in worship for the benefit of an "outsider." This word seems to suggest that this person does not have gifts of the Spirit. That would mean,

While the weekly corporate gathering of the saints, where we together choose to exalt Christ, is the ideal, all too often, the church is tempted to promote an experience or program over authentic gathering. When church becomes oriented around an experience or simply a program, inevitably it becomes about the individual preference rather than the person of Christ. Jared Wilson, in his book *The Prodigal Church*, highlighted the tension well.

> The weekend church gathering is never seen in the Scriptures as a place where individuals go to enjoy a particular experience, nor as the central place of evangelism. . . . If you treat the worship gathering as an experiential production . . . the church begins to see itself as concert-goers or, again, as customers rather than as the body of Christ.
>
> The worship service, biblically, is a gathering of Christians to enjoy God in communion with him and each other. . . . [T]he service is meant to reorient the body around its head—Jesus Christ—and to prepare us for the ongoing personal and communal witness of the church outside the gathering.[14]

Because we look for an experience, we have been conditioned to come expecting something from the church gathering, versus expecting to contribute to the church gathering. For example, do we come looking for others to engage us, or do we come looking to engage others? Do we seek out, or are we waiting to be sought out? I regularly have conversations with people who have left their churches. They frequently tell me that they do not feel and have not felt connected to others in the church in years. They talk about coming and sitting in church and feeling disconnected and alone. I always ask them:

- "How many people did you invite over to your home?"
- "Where were you serving in the church?"
- "In the church, with whom were you engaging, in whom were you investing?"

---

of course, that he or she is an unbeliever. The passage reads, "Therefore, one who speaks in a tongue should pray that he may interpret. For if I pray in a tongue, my spirit prays but my mind is unfruitful. What am I to do? I will pray with my spirit, but I will pray with my mind also; I will sing praise with my spirit, but I will sing with my mind also. Otherwise, if you give thanks with your spirit, how can anyone in the position of an outsider say 'Amen' to your thanksgiving when he does not know what you are saying?" (vv. 13–16). One aspect of Paul's concern with the abuse and inappropriate exaltation of the gift of tongues in the Corinthian church was the confusion it created for lost people who might be present in a public, corporate church service. Paul seemed to expect lost people to be present, and expected the Corinthian congregants to acknowledge the practicality of his argument. The church worship service should be reasonably intelligible to those outside of the church, so that they can hear and respond to the message.

[14] Jared C. Wilson, *The Prodigal Church* (Wheaton, IL: Crossway, 2015), 62.

In other words, I am asking them whether they were *gathering* or just *showing up*.

Community and relationships take time, and they take work. We must be willing to put in that work. These gatherings provide the platform for authentic community to take place, but it does take time and hard work. Brett McCracken, in his book *Uncomfortable*, insightfully remarked that being the church is all about "looking outside of ourselves" and "putting aside personal comfort and coming often to the cross."[15] When we have a "gathering" mentality, church becomes more about encouraging others and exalting Christ and so much less about us. The church is called to gather together, focusing on Christ weekly for the purpose of equipping and encouragement so that we can then go engage a lost and broken world together. We gather together to prepare us to join Jesus on his mission of reconciliation (2 Cor 5:11–21).

A Biblical Church Gathers Continually

The second mode of gathering is to gather continually. As we stated previously, Sunday morning is not the only time we are the church. Sunday prepares us to go and be the church in our everyday lives. We come, worship, and encourage one another to be the church throughout the week, and we should be regularly engaging one another day by day in preparation for the next all-inclusive gathering. So while we do gather on Sunday, our time together does not end there. We should seek to constantly gather and engage one another as we see the early church doing in Acts 2:

> And *all who believed were together* and had all things in common. And they were selling their possessions and belongings and distributing the proceeds to all, as any had need. And *day by day*, attending the temple *together and breaking bread in their homes*, they received their food with glad and generous hearts, praising God and having favor with all the people. And the Lord added to their number day by day those who were being saved. (vv. 44–47)

Notice, the early church was constantly gathering together and investing in one another's lives. These were not all formal gatherings. These believers were

---

[15]   Brett McCracken, *Uncomfortable: The Awkward and Essential Challenge of Christian Community* (Wheaton, IL: Crossway, 2017), 39.

simply involved with and invested in one another throughout the week on a regular basis. They were together, met in each other's homes, and did these things day by day.

Like the early church, we, too, should gather together on Sundays for fellowship, celebration, and so on, but in addition to our structured corporate gathering time, we are also called to gather regularly throughout the week to engage one another while engaging the world. Let's spend time together, both to build one another up and to reach others for the cause of Christ.

Interestingly, these early-church Christians were still regularly going to the temple together. Why? By this time, they already knew that Jesus was the ultimate priest and sacrifice (Heb 7:23–28). He was their promised Messiah. Their sins had been forgiven by God through Christ. There was no longer a need for the rituals of the temple; nevertheless, they continued to go. This point will be explored more fully in chapter 5, but for now, it is sufficient to say that the temple was where people were. It was the heart of their city and culture. The temple was where the church went to engage those who had yet to believe the gospel. This practice of cultural engagement within the Jewish religious centers is further evidenced in Paul's missionary approach. As Paul traveled away from Jerusalem, where the temple was located, he would go into the Jewish synagogues with others and engage those present with the gospel until he was forced out. What we see in Acts 2 is that these early believers are going to the temple in community along with the apostles and influencing others for the cause of Jesus. And they are doing it together.[16]

There is another interesting feature often overlooked in this text. The church is breaking bread and gathering regularly in homes over meals. Part of what this passage is calling us to is a radical hospitality, an opening of our homes to others for the purpose of ministering to one another and connecting. Rosaria Butterfield spoke of hospitality this way: "Radically ordinary hospitality—those who live it see strangers as neighbors and neighbors as family of God. . . . Those who live out radically ordinary hospitality see their homes not as theirs but as God's gift to use for the furtherance of his kingdom."[17] This is what we are called to as Christians: radically ordinary hospitality. At the heart of such hospitality is an understanding that we are not our own, and all we have is open for others and to be used as God sees fit. Luke was clear to explain that this was the disposition of their hearts. After all, in addition to sharing their

---

[16] One such scene is in Acts 3:1–9, where Peter and John engaged a lame beggar.
[17] Rosaria Butterfield, *The Gospel Comes with a House Key: Practicing Radically Ordinary Hospitality in Our Post-Christian World* (Wheaton, IL: Crossway, 2018), 11.

food with others, which came at a cost, "all who believed were together and had all things in common. And they were selling their possessions and belongings and distributing the proceeds to all, as any had need" (Acts 2:44–45).

Acts 2 ends with an affirmation of the Lord's faithfulness as believers were obedient and lived out kingdom values together. The Lord added to their number day by day. People were coming to believe in Jesus when his community lived counterculturally and cared more for one another than for themselves while engaging the world around them. The world saw something different in this community: something that set them apart. The Spirit of Jesus had transformed this community and changed their selfish desires into unselfish ones. Could it be that one reason our churches are not more effective in reaching the world around them is because we have shifted our focus off of these kingdom concepts that are to be present in our corporate and continual gathering?

Beyond the undeniable fact that God expects the body of believers to be gathering, there are a number of benefits to regularly gathering and engaging one another throughout the week. When we seek to gather regularly, we will find temptation restrained and community developed.

Two Benefits of Gathering Continually

Temptation Is Restrained
Several years ago, I (Adam) had to get a CT scan for some pain in my jaw to rule out the possibility of a tumor. The clinic where the test was to be performed was a two-and-a-half-hour car ride away. Knowing in advance that this appointment was upcoming, I called a friend and asked if he wanted to go with me since he was home nursing his own injury. He agreed. So, on the day of the appointment, I picked him up, and we drove to the clinic together. We talked about all kinds of stuff along the way as we discussed our injuries, our faith, our families, and all types of interests and hobbies we had. On our way back, we decided to grab lunch, where our conversation flourished even more. Afterward, I finished driving him the rest of the way home, and then I headed home myself.

Now, guess what? The whole time I was with my friend, I did not experience any temptation to sin. The entire time I was gone from home and away from the city, not one time was I tempted to give in to road rage, yell at the poor soul who took the parking spot we wanted, overeat at lunch, speed or neglect to use my turn signal, brood over an unkind remark someone had made, focus on past painful situations or anything like that. Why? Because someone who holds me to a higher standard than that was with me. A brother in the Lord Jesus Christ was with me. A member of the church was keeping me accountable by simply being there. His presence helped curb temptation. Why is this the case? It is because one of the major benefits of meeting together continually is this: Christian community restrains sin! Not only did it restrain sin, but having my friend there reminded me to be more kind and patient and gracious. We are influenced by the community with whom we are connecting. A good church community encourages us not only away from sin, but also toward righteousness.

I have noticed something about my family when my wife and I have visitors over to our home or when we are out to eat. When others are present, we are more likely to talk kindly to each other and to be more balanced in the discipline of our children. What about you? Why is that? It is because we are more gracious when other people are around. The presence of other people restrains our fleshly desires, our natural impulses. The right kind of people produce accountability by merely being there. As an aside, the flip side of this reality is also true. The wrong crowd can stimulate sinful tendencies. Our communal environment influences us for good or bad. The community with whom you choose to gather will either encourage or restrain sin. This idea is important as we think about influencing our communities. We, as the church, want to be the kind of community that restrains sin and encourages righteousness. One of the keys to creating such a community is to be faithful and consistent in gathering corporately and continually. When we are faithful and consistent in gathering as believers, we are being trained to be the kind of Christians, the kind of community, that will restrain sin and encourage righteousness.

Community Is Developed

So far in this chapter, the word *engage* has been mostly used of an action taken by the church toward the world. We are to engage the world with the gospel, as we'll see in chapter 5. Here, we want to take a moment and clarify an important concept regarding engaging one another as believers.

"Gathering" is not a passive activity. When the church gathers, it gathers with a purpose: to contribute to community, not just to have a personal experience. As the church gathers, whether corporately or informally during the week, its members need to engage one another. We must not just idly gather; we should participate together in meaningful ways, to create the community God intended us to be. An intentionality should be evident in our gathering.

Let us go back for a moment and revisit Hebrews 10. The author of Hebrews believed intentional gathering was essential, as evidenced by the command he gave the church: "And let us consider how to stir up one another to love and good works" (v. 24). In other words, let's think about how we can live out the confession of faith we have in Jesus (v. 23), and let us implement a practical way to do this in community. How? How can we as believers continue to promote love and good works in each other's lives? The writer, under the inspiration of the Holy Spirit, said we could fulfill this amazing goal by "not neglecting to meet together, as is the habit of some, but encouraging one another, and all the more as you see the Day drawing near" (v. 25). As we meet, we do so to actively engage the other members of the body of Jesus so that we might encourage one another to live out the gospel faithfully in anticipation of Jesus coming back. It is in this meaningful engagement that community is founded, developed, and maintained. This "community" is the second major benefit of meeting together continually. When we meet with such intentionality, community is developed and maintained.

Intentional gathering can relate to both our more formal, corporate times and our casual gatherings throughout the week—anytime believers in Christ meet together explicitly to minister to one another in the name of Jesus. Here is an example of a casual gathering experience.

I (Adam) remember when a good friend of mine moved into the Louisville area. He had been in Ohio and was relocating about six months ahead of his family. He stayed in a hotel I was managing. During that time, I would occasionally check up on him, go to eat lunch with him, and ask him questions, like these:

- "How are you protecting your thought life and marriage while away from your family?"
- "How are you doing in your walk with Christ?"
- "Is your job just a job or is it a calling?"
- "How are you handling loneliness?"

As a result of those conversations, we built a great friendship that lasts until this day, but, more so, it is a friendship we will be able to celebrate together in the kingdom of heaven. Why did I meet with him and ask him those kinds of personal questions? I did so because I knew that if I were in a similar situation I would want and need someone to ask me those kinds of questions. Gathering continually, whether corporately or casually, is designed by God to restrain sin and build community.

Final Thoughts

Let us think about our engagement with our church community. When someone in our church has a spouse go out of town, do we call him and ask him how he is doing? Does he need anything? Do we go by? Do we ask him if he is maintaining his purity and keeping his mind on the things of Christ? Do we pray with him over the phone or swing by to pray in person?

When someone is particularly needy or a chronic complainer, do we avoid her as a nuisance, or do we engage her as someone who matters and who is valuable in the eyes of God?

Do we see ourselves as fellow ministers of Jesus to the body, or do we believe the only minister is the pastor, bishop, or priest? Do we invite people to go with us fishing, golfing, shopping, to the movies, or out for dinner? Do we take time to just hang out with other believers? Spending time with other believers offers a great chance to invite an unbeliever to hang with you as you gather.

When someone shares a prayer request, do we try to follow up with her? When someone does not show up for the church service for a couple of weeks, do we call and check up on him? Do we even notice when he is missing? When people gather with us corporately, do we encourage them in Christ?

Moreover, Christ's church is called to be an actively gathering church. Are you gathering? Are you engaging? Imagine the difference it would make if when people came to your church gathering, they were engaged for the cause of Christ. Imagine if we all collectively, especially the mature among us, saw Sunday as a ministry time during which we engaged others and encouraged them in their walk with Jesus. Imagine if Sundays were intentionally a time during which we came expecting to focus our hearts and minds on Jesus, and we prayed before arriving, "Lord, show me who to encourage today and how to encourage them, and help me to fix my eyes more firmly on Jesus, the author and perfecter of my faith." Imagine if we promoted our churches by saying, not, "You'll have a great experience!" but, "You will encounter great people worshiping a great God!" What would such a church be like? I have a feeling it would look an awful lot like the early church.

Personal Reflection or
Group Discussion Questions

1. Before reading this chapter, how did you think about the gathering of the church? How has your thinking changed?

2. Do you attend a local church? What is the purpose of the church? Are you contributing to that purpose?

3. When your church gathers corporately, what elements of worship do you see truly affecting your life? How are you engaged in the church? If you are not, how could you get involved? How do you use your gifts to edify (build up) the body of Christ? If you do not, how could you begin to do so?

4. When have you been more concerned with the experience of church than the faithfulness of the church? Do you promote the faithfulness of the church or the experiential benefits to someone when you talk about your church? When going to church, do you seek what is comfortable for you or what is good for the body and that which exalts Christ?

5. Are you involved in gathering continually with some members of your church? If so, how has this community contributed to your life as part of the body of Christ? If not, how could getting involved with a small group benefit you or the rest of the body of Christ?

6. Church people are sometimes known to gather for idle talk and no real action. How can we engage one another in truly meaningful ways? What effect does Christian community really have?

Devotional

Day One: Acts 2:42–47

Have you experienced true community? Where did you experience it? What characterized it?

Open your Bible and read Acts 2:42–47. In this passage, Luke, the author of the book of Acts, described how the new Christian community was functioning and what spirit and attitude characterized it.

Think deeply about the following questions:

Have you experienced a community that functions as Luke describes or is characterized by such an attitude? Is your church community like this one?

If you have not seen this kind of community in your church, you could be the catalyst that God will use to awaken this kind of biblical and faithful community in your local church. How can you practically have "all things in common" with members of your church community? How can you practically "day by day, attend the temple together and break bread" with one another?

If you have seen this kind of community in your church and are not involved, why aren't you? Are you being selfish? Are you afraid to open yourself and your life up to the transparency of true community?

If you are involved in this kind of community, what have its effects been in your life?

In this passage, what is the result of the community of God's people loving each other the way that they should? What does this say about the way our churches practice community?

How can you make preparations this week to be in community with others?

Devotional

Day Two: Titus 2:1–15

Have you ever confronted someone about something? How did you feel? Have you ever been confronted? How did that feel? Have you ever been confronted by a mentor or someone else whom you greatly respect?

Open your Bible and read Titus 2:1–15.

In this passage, Paul is writing to his mentee, Titus, describing how fellowship and accountability are to be ingrained in the very structure and ministry of the local congregation.

Think deeply about the following questions:

What does Paul's description of the roles of older men and older women show about the community? What exactly was their role? Why does this matter?

Paul specifically said to Titus, "Show yourself in all respects to be a model of good works, and in your teaching show integrity, dignity, and sound speech that cannot be condemned, so that an opponent may be put to shame, having nothing evil to say about us" (2:7, 8). How can this be applied to every member of the community? Do you live this way? What resources does the good news of the gospel give us to help us live this way?

Why did the conduct of bondservants matter to Paul? How would the lives of slaves/servants change when they came to know Jesus? How would they fit into the community of faith?

What motivation did Paul give at the end of the passage for living as he has directed?

How can you be involved in rhythms of accountability and fellowship in your church context if you are not already?

Devotional

Day Three: Hebrews 10:19–25

Think of a time when you encouraged a friend or were significantly encouraged by a friend. What happened? How did it feel?

Open your Bible and read Hebrews 10:19–25.

In this passage, the author of Hebrews drew an argument to a conclusion by encouraging his listeners that Jesus is truly great.

Think deeply about the following questions:

According to this passage and its context in the book, how can we be so confident and assured of our salvation?

Jesus is faithful! Because of this, we can have faith and hope in him. What does it look like to hold fast to our confession of hope without wavering?

What is our motivation to "stir up one another to love and good works"? What does that mean, really, and what are some practical ways to do so?

This passage makes not meeting together the opposite of encouraging one other. Why is that? What are some practical ways to encourage others?

Why is it increasingly important to "stir up one another to love and good works" as we see the Day—that is, the return of Jesus—approaching?

Devotional

Day Four: 1 Timothy 4:6–16

Have you ever tried to get in shape? Maybe you went to the gym regularly, joined an exercise class, or got a personal trainer. What was your experience?

Open your Bible and read 1 Timothy 4:6–16.

In this passage, Paul wrote to his friend and colleague, Timothy, to encourage him to train for godliness and to train the congregation for godliness as well.

Think deeply about the following questions:

What does it look like to train for godliness? How are training for godliness and good doctrine connected, and how should they inform each other? Why is training for godliness valuable both for us and for those we are in community with?

What is our motivation for training for godliness? What hinders your training for godliness?

Paul told Timothy specifically to "set the believers an example in speech, in conduct, in love, in faith, in purity." Why is an example of these behaviors so important? Likewise, what type of example have your own actions been for those around you this week?

Paul tells Timothy to "devote [himself] to the public reading of Scripture, to exhortation, to teaching." What implication does this have for the church when it gathers? Paul also discussed the fact that Timothy had a gift of the Spirit and that his gift should not be neglected. What implication does that have for the church when it gathers?

How can you prepare for this week's gathering of the church? How do you keep from neglecting the gift God has given you?

Devotional

Day Five: Luke 9:1–6 and Matthew 10:1–13

Have you ever been commissioned for a task? How did it feel to bear that responsibility?

Open your Bible and read Luke 9:1–6 and Matthew 10:1–13.

In this chapter, we discussed the church being a true community. One way the church has done this is by meeting in one another's homes. In these two passages from the Gospels, we see that the precedent for meeting with one another in homes was set by Jesus when he commissioned his disciples.

Think deeply about the following questions:

What might these passages have to say about our hospitality as a community?

What seems to be Jesus's goal as he sends out his disciples? What should be our goal as we open our homes?

How can you open your home to others this week?

How does the teaching of Jesus and Paul line up or diverge? How should this affect the way we love our neighbors and other members of our church community? How can we invite others into our church community?

CHAPTER 3

PRAYING CHURCH:
We Submit to God

Prayer was a central characteristic of the early church. According to Acts 2,

> And they *devoted themselves to* the apostles' teaching and the fellow-ship, to the breaking of bread and *the prayers*. And awe came upon every soul, and many wonders and signs were being done through the apostles. And all who believed were together and had all things in common. And they were selling their possessions and belongings and distributing the proceeds to all, as any had need. And day by day, attending the temple together and breaking bread in their homes, they received their food with glad and generous hearts, praising God and having favor with all the people. And the Lord added to their number day by day those who were being saved. (vv. 42–47)

God acts throughout the narrative of the Bible for his own glory. He often does this in powerful and dramatic ways. For instance, think of God creating the universe out of nothing, flooding the whole world while saving a faithful remnant, launching the plagues at faithless Egypt, splitting the Red Sea, and raising the valley of dry bones. Though these acts were mighty indeed, some of God's most compelling actions are also some of the most personal and come as a result of the prayers of his people. Consider an example from 1 Samuel.

The Biblical Precedent for Prayer

Hannah was one of two wives of a man named Elkanah. Though Hannah was barren, Elkanah's other wife, Peninnah, had many children, and she shamed and ridiculed Hannah for her inability to measure up. In anguish, Hannah prayed these words to God: "O Lord of hosts, if you will indeed look on the affliction of your servant and remember me and not forget your servant, but will give to your servant a son, then I will give him to the Lord all the days of his life, and no razor shall touch his head" (1 Sam 1:11). The Lord indeed answered her prayer, and her son Samuel went on to become a very important prophet in Israel's history. In addition to answering her prayer with Samuel, the Lord blessed Hannah with five *more* children. God acts when his people pray.

Hezekiah, king of Judah, prayed fervently for the Lord to break the Assyrian siege against Jerusalem: "Truly, O Lord, the kings of Assyria have laid waste the nations and their lands and have cast their gods into the fire, for they were not gods, but the work of men's hands, wood and stone. Therefore, they were destroyed. So now, O Lord our God, save us, please, from his hand, that all the kingdoms of the earth may know that you, O Lord, are God alone" (2 Kgs 19:17–19). In response to this prayer, the angel of the Lord killed 85,000 Assyrian soldiers and broke the siege. The rest of the enemy army fled. God acts when his people pray.

Jairus, one of the rulers of the synagogue in Jerusalem, came to Jesus with a simple plea: "My little daughter is at the point of death. Come and lay your hands on her, so that she may be made well and live" (Mark 5:23).[1] On the way to Jairus's house, Jesus stopped to heal another woman. By the time he arrived at Jairus's house, the man's daughter had died; however, because of Jairus's faith, Jesus raised his daughter from the dead.

In Acts 12, the apostle Peter was imprisoned, yet the church earnestly prayed for him (v. 5). In response to those prayers, God sent an angel and miraculously delivered Peter from prison. God acts when we pray in faith.

Now, does God always answer prayers in such dramatic fashion? No, but he sometimes does. Even beyond the reality of dramatic answers, we know that God hears and delights in the prayers of his righteous people (Prov 15:8, 29).

---

[1]   In this context, one could argue that this scenario is not a prayer; rather, it is Jairus speaking face-to-face with Jesus, but is that not what we are doing in prayer? Are we not entering into a dialogue? The issue in prayer is not the distance of our communication, whether face-to-face or between the realities of earth and heaven. Instead, the issue in prayer is our submission to and reliance upon God. It is acknowledging in faith the greatness of God, our desperate need for God, and our submission to his ultimately good purposes. For more on the necessity of faith in prayer and the effectual nature of faith-based prayers, see Jas 5:13–18.

James goes on to tell us that the faith-filled prayers of a righteous person are powerful and effective (Jas 5:16).

Nineteenth-century revivalist E. M. Bounds made a bold statement regarding prayer and the church that is still relevant:

> The church today needs praying men to execute her solemn and pressing responsibility to meet the fearful crisis which is facing her. The crying need of the times is for . . . God-fearing men, praying men, Holy-Ghost men, men who can endure hardship, who will count not their lives dear unto themselves, but count all things but dross for the excellency of the knowledge of Jesus Christ, the Savior. The men who are so greatly needed in this age of the church are those who have learned the business of praying—learned it on their knees, learned it in the need and agony of their own hearts.[2]

A critical challenge of the church today is its need to be a praying church. Prayer is a privileged conversation with God. Prayer from a humble, God-honoring saint is a powerful weapon. Anyone can become a courageous, confident, consistent prayer warrior, and God has called his church to live in constant conversation, seeking him amid all things and at all times (1 Thess 5:17).

The activity of prayer was an evidential characteristic of the early church. As Luke revealed in Acts 2:42, "They devoted themselves to the apostles' teaching and the fellowship, to the breaking of bread and the prayers." We in the church today tend to elevate those who serve, but all too often, the unsung heroes of the church are those who faithfully pray. Prayer matters, and we are called to be a praying church, both corporately and individually.

Charles Spurgeon and Prayer

Charles Spurgeon, who died in 1892 at the age of fifty-seven, is often remembered in the Christian community as the "Prince of Preachers." While volumes have been written about his life, he is most commonly known for his pastoral ministry at the Metropolitan Tabernacle, where he preached to packed crowds of thousands without any means of voice amplification. His sermons sold thousands of copies weekly around the world. The popularity of

---

[2] E. M. Bounds, *The Best of E. M. Bounds on Prayer* (Grand Rapids: Baker Books, 1981), 146–47.

his preaching endures even today. As the name "Prince of Preachers" suggests, he is well known for his powerful and eloquent sermons, yet it has been suggested that although he loved to preach, Spurgeon foremost considered himself a man of prayer. He credited his success to the faithful prayers of the people in his church. He told his students in the college he led, "We may discover, after having laboured long and wearily in preaching, that all the honour belongs to another builder, whose prayers were gold, silver, and precious stones, while our sermonizing, being apart from prayer, were but hay and stubble."[3] He understood that the church is not a platform for a charismatic leader, but a body made of many equal parts with different functions. It has been reported that he would often tell people, "I always give all the glory to God, but I do not forget that He gave me the privilege of ministering from the first to a praying people. We had prayer meetings . . . that moved our very souls. Every man seemed like a crusader besieging the New Jerusalem. Each one appeared determined to storm the Celestial City by the might of intercession."[4]

There is an oft-repeated story that has persisted over the years that reinforces Spurgeon's appreciation for the prayers of the church.[5] It has been reported that one day some college students were sightseeing in London when they decided to hear the famed C. H. Spurgeon preach. After arriving early, they were sitting and talking among themselves when a man from the congregation came by and greeted them. After an exchange of pleasant conversation, he said, "Gentlemen, let me show you around. Would you like to see the heating plant of this church?" The young men were not particularly interested; nevertheless, not wanting to offend the hospitable stranger, they agreed. The young men were taken inside and down a stairway. Quietly, a door was opened, and their guide whispered, "This is our heating plant." Surprised, the students saw hundreds of people quietly bowed in prayer, seeking a blessing on the service that was soon to begin above in the auditorium. Closing the door, the gentleman then introduced himself. It was none other than Charles Haddon Spurgeon.

Even as a great preacher who was constantly commanding the attention of audiences, Spurgeon was humble, in part, because he knew that the Holy Spirit enabled his ministry through prayer. Spurgeon was not the one primarily acting and effecting change in the church; the Spirit was moving in response to the

---

3   Charles H. Spurgeon, *Lectures to My Students: A Selection from Addresses Delivered to the Students of the Pastors' College, Metropolitan Tabernacle* (London: Passmore & Alabaster, 1875), 1:46.

4   Daniel Partner, ed. *The Essential Works of Charles Spurgeon: Selected Books, Sermons, and Other Writings* (Uhrichsville, OH: Barbour, 2009), 94.

5   We could not verify the origin of this story, but found it in several sources; therefore, it has been reproduced here.

prayers of God's people. Prayer was of supreme importance to Spurgeon and his church because they knew they needed the Lord to move.

Acts 4:24–30 as a Model for Prayer

Our hope for this chapter is threefold. We hope that by the end you will

- be reminded that prayer is to be part of the identity and action of the church,
- come away with a renewed commitment to pray, and
- come away with a renewed understanding of ways to pray.

There are many reasons given in the Bible for why people pray, as well as many models for prayer. For now, we are going to focus on one revealed in Acts 4. In this passage, Peter and John are arrested and threatened for proclaiming the gospel and healing a crippled man in Jesus's name (vv. 3, 21). Luke then goes on to describe the details of their release and the response of their fellow believers.

When they were released, they went to their friends and reported what the chief priests and the elders had said to them. And when they heard it, they lifted their voices together to God and said, "Sovereign Lord, who made the heaven and the earth and the sea and everything in them, who through the mouth of our father David, your servant, said by the Holy Spirit,

"'Why did the Gentiles rage,
    and the peoples plot in vain?
The kings of the earth set themselves,
    and the rulers were gathered together,
    against the Lord and against his Anointed'—

for truly in this city there were gathered together against your holy servant Jesus, whom you anointed, both Herod and Pontius Pilate, along with the Gentiles and the peoples of Israel, to do whatever your hand and your plan had predestined to take place. And now, Lord, look upon their threats and grant to your servants to continue to speak your word with all boldness, while you stretch out your hand to heal, and signs and wonders are performed through the name of your holy servant Jesus." And when they had prayed, the place in which they were gathered together was shaken, and they were all filled with the Holy Spirit and continued to speak the word of God with boldness. (Acts 4:23–31)

Can you imagine the scene? How amazing! In response to persecution, the church prayed. Not only did they pray, but God also responded positively to their prayer. He showed up in a big way. Why? In part, because of the elements of their prayer. Prayers in the Bible can serve as models for us as we seek to be the type of praying church God desires. To that end, let us examine four elements of their prayer that might be instrumental in shaping our prayers.

They Addressed God as He Has Been Revealed
First, the apostles addressed God as he had revealed himself to them, and not based on their own inclinations. The opening of their prayer is recorded in v. 24: "Sovereign Lord, who made the heaven and the earth and the sea and everything in them . . ." The apostles addressed God as the sovereign Lord and the Creator God. He is the one who is sovereign over all, and he is the one who has created all. The apostles knew to designate God this way because God had attributed these characteristics to himself in the Old Testament, and they had been students of the Scriptures. They were familiar with God's self-revelation, and they used it as a guide in their prayers. Knowing how God has revealed himself and using revelation as a guide for addressing God is important.

Several years ago, I (Adam) was meeting weekly with a group of men after church on Wednesday nights. These men had come to me and wanted me to disciple them in theology. One particular Wednesday night, I posed this question to begin our meeting: "Is it okay to pray to God as Mother?" Over the next several minutes, I sat back and listened to the individual men share and defend with one another a variety of answers to this question. Some answers were provided in support of praying to God as Mother, and some were against it. Finally, I intervened and decided to press this important point concerning God's self-revelation, offering the following argument.

We know that God is not a man, but *how* do we know that? We know it, not merely based on our experiences or preferences, but based on what God has revealed about himself in the Bible. The prophet Balaam declared in Num 23:19, "God is not man . . . or a son of man." Balaam's point, in part, was that God is not human, frail, or capable of corrupt action. God is divine. He is holy and perfect. He is the Creator of humankind. Jesus himself declared that "God is spirit" (John 4:24). God is not bound to a corporeal existence. Notwithstanding, God at times provided a self-description in human terms. Sometimes this description involved bodily elements for the purpose of communicating a divine point. For example, God's "*hand* is not shortened, that it cannot save" (Isa 59:1), "the *eyes* of the LORD run to and fro throughout the whole earth, to give strong support to those whose heart is blameless toward him" (2 Chr 16:9), and "Man shall not live by bread alone, but by every word that comes from the *mouth* of God" (Matt 4:4).[6] Since God chose to provide a self-description, it is important that we look at it. Several passages reveal that God has chosen to present himself as "Father."[7] The prophecy of Jer 3:19 revealed, "'And I thought you would call me, My Father, and would not turn from following me." Isaiah declared, "But now, O LORD, you are our Father; we are the clay, and you are our potter" (Isa 64:8). Jesus, when teaching his disciples to pray, affirmed this position, crying out, "Our Father in heaven . . ." (Matt 6:9).

These statements concerning the fatherhood of God do not mean that God is not described with any maternal qualities;[8] they simply demonstrate that when God disclosed himself to people, he did so with the title "Father" and the pronoun "he" and is never revealed as "Mother" or "she."[9] Again, God does not have a physical anatomy, per se. This point is that the way God has chosen to reveal himself to us should guide how we address him. We should address God in a manner consistent with his self-revelation and not based on our own inclinations and preferences.[10]

Prayer needs to start here: addressing God as he has revealed himself. We

---

[6]   Many other examples can be found in the Bible (Exod 6:6; Num 6:25; Ps 34:15; 44:2–3; etc.). Such descriptions are known as "anthropomorphisms." An anthropomorphism is a literary device wherein a human feature or action is attributed to God.

[7]   Here are a few such passages: 2 Sam 7:14; 1 Chr 17:13; Ps 89:26; Isa 63:16; Jer 3:19; Mal 2:10; Matt 6:26; Luke 11:2, 13; 1 Cor 8:6; 2 Cor 1:3; 1 John 1:3.

[8]   Here are a few such passages: Deut 32:11–12; Hos 13:8; Matt 23:37.

[9]   The passage that probably gets closest to referencing God as Mother is Isa 66:13, which reads, "As one whom his mother comforts, so I will comfort you; you shall be comforted in Jerusalem." However, this verse is a simile comparing God's actions to those of a loving mother. It is not attributing a self-disclosed title as do 1 Chr 17:13; Ps 89:26; and Luke 11:2.

[10]   God's self-disclosure as Father also speaks to the culture in which the Bible was written and helps us understand the beauty of redemption and the reality of sonship. God as Father sending his Son, Jesus, so that we could become "sons" of God speaks to the deep spiritual truth regarding the inheritance we as children of God now have in and through Christ.

should come to God with respect and honor, as he is the Creator and sovereign King. God's kingly status does not rule out that he is our Father; in fact, it is just as true and even more amazing that the sovereign Lord and King is also our loving Father, with whom we can express emotion and seek an audience at any time. It is because of this loving relationship that we should respect him and love him by submitting to his authority and addressing him as he has disclosed himself to us. Prayer should start by addressing God as he has revealed himself in his revelation: the Bible. Not only did the early church pray this way, but they went further and used Scripture as a means of praying to God.

They Started with Scripture

There is a story you may have heard before, typically attributed to Paul Harvey, about a three-year-old boy who was tagging along with his mother to the grocery store. Before entering the store, the boy's mother sternly warned him, "Now, you're not going to get any chocolate chip cookies, so don't even ask." She put him in the cart, and he sat in the child's seat while she wheeled down the aisles. He was doing fine until they came to the cookie section. When he saw the chocolate chip cookies, he turned in the seat and said to her, "Mom, can I have some chocolate chip cookies?" She reminded him, "I told you not to even ask. You're not going to get any today." Later, the mother realized she had forgotten an item on her list. Her pursuits inevitably led her back down the cookie aisle.

"Mom, can I please have some chocolate chip cookies?" the boy pleaded.

"I told you that you can't have any today. Now, don't ask me again."

Finally, they approached the checkout lane. The little boy sensed this was his last chance, so just before they got to the line, he bowed his head and cried out in his loudest voice, "In the name of Jesus, may I have some chocolate chip cookies?" Everyone around them laughed. Some even applauded, and, due to the generosity of the other shoppers, the little boy and his mother left with twenty-three boxes of chocolate chip cookies.[11]

How often is this how we see prayer, where we just slap the name of Jesus on the front of self-indulgent demands to make it more likely we will get what we want? Sadly, this is not a Christian understanding of prayer, but rather a pagan one. In the ancient pagan world, sacrifices and prayers were offered to deities with the goal of manipulating them to do what the people desired. People would do for the god whatever they thought would get the

---

[11] This story has appeared in numerous illustrations over the years; however, we were unable to confirm the actual origin or when it was originally told.

desired result.[12] They would offer one sacrifice for a good harvest and another sacrifice for fertile wives. In fact, it is well documented that in pagan religion "self-interest is intrinsic to the setting" of "supplications and prayers."[13] In reality, these men and women were worshiping themselves: their own desires and supposed needs became their gods. How often do we, as Christians, do the very same thing? When we do this, we are not praying in a manner that has been revealed in Scripture, but are actually following the selfish pagan practices of the ancient world. No wonder we have no confidence in our prayers. When we pray for self-indulgent reasons, our prayers have no power (Jas 1:6; 4:3). However, when we pray for that which we know God already wants in our lives, we have great power and confidence.

This is where Scripture comes in. Scripture helps us see what it is that God wants. It helps us understand how God has worked in the lives of his people in the past and instructs us in our walk with him today. Scripture reminds us of who God is and who we are in light of who he is. It helps us pray in a manner consistent with the pattern that has been laid out before us. For these reasons, and many others, it is important for us to be both in the Word and saturated by the Word. When we saturate our hearts with Scripture, we are more likely to be moved to speak God's Word back to him. The Holy Spirit will not draw water from a well that has not been dug. We cannot expect Scripture to flow into and through our prayers if we are not committed to spending time in the Bible. When we get inside the Word of God and meditate deeply on its truths, we begin to change. The Spirit of God uses prayer and Scripture reading in tandem with living in community with God's people to transform us into the kind of people who love God and desire him.

It is interesting that the early church in Acts 4, in their moment of need, went to God in prayer and took time to speak God's Word back to him. Prayer was important to them, and the way they prayed should be instructive to us. They prayed a portion of Scripture that was relevant to their current situation. In their prayer, they quoted Ps 2:1–2 (italicized in the following text):

> Sovereign Lord, . . . who through the mouth of our father David, your servant, said by the Holy Spirit, *Why did the Gentiles rage, and the peoples plot in vain? The kings of the earth set themselves, and the rulers were gathered together, against the Lord and against his Anointed*— for truly in this city there were gathered together against your holy

---

[12]   An Old Testament example of this practice is found in 1 Kgs 18:25–29.

[13]   John H. Walton, *Ancient Near Eastern Thought and the Old Testament* (Grand Rapids: Baker Academic, 2006), 146.

servant Jesus, whom you anointed, both Herod and Pontius Pilate, along with the Gentiles and the peoples of Israel. (Acts 4:24–27)

Several important details emerge as we look at how they utilized this passage in their prayer.

By reflecting on and citing this passage the way they did, they acknowledged that these writings were not merely the words of David, but the words of God given through David. They were affirming the inspiration of Scripture.[14] In other words, they recognized they were praying God's Word back to him. They reminded themselves collectively and reminded God of the promises of his Word.

They were also allowing this text to point them to Jesus. The church saw Jesus's suffering in light of David's suffering. Jesus suffered persecution at the hands of the nations in the tradition of David. The early church was able to identify that just as David, God's anointed leader of his people, suffered at the hands of the nations, so Jesus, God's only Son and eternal King, suffered at the hands of the nations to bring redemption to his people. They were able to identify with the struggles of both David and Jesus and see that in suffering on behalf of his people, Jesus bought their redemption.

In addition, their prayer from Psalm 2 affirms that God's people have always been persecuted. By appropriating the words of a suffering David for themselves, they communicated to God that they were in the same position his people have been in before and that they trusted God would be faithful to them just as he had been faithful to his people in the past. These saints not only saw David's suffering in Jesus, but they saw both in their current suffering. Not only were they confident God would be faithful to them just as he was faithful to David (and Jesus), but they understood that Jesus could identify with them in their own suffering because he had already suffered on their behalf. Jesus, the Suffering Servant, who laid down his life for his people, is intimately familiar with our pain. As the author of Hebrews wrote, "For we do not have a high priest who is unable to sympathize with our weaknesses, but one who in every respect has been tempted as we are, yet without sin. Let us then with confidence draw near to the throne of grace, that we may receive mercy and find grace to help in time of need" (Heb 4:15–16). In praying these words to God, the early church declared this same truth. Kelly Kapic captured it this way:

---

[14]   The Christian doctrine of inspiration is an important one. Verbal plenary inspiration is the doctrine that every word of Scripture is exactly as God intended. This doctrine affirms that the Holy Spirit of God inspired the human authors to write the original manuscripts while preserving the personality and style of the individual writers.

Jesus points us forward to a new hope, a new life. God achieves the new in us not by obliterating the old but by entering our situation, taking it for his own, and then transforming it. . . . The Son of God has taken on flesh, has felt physical pain, and has even entered the unutterable darkness of death itself . . . But Jesus will be more than merely sympathetic. The incarnate Son comes from the Father and in the Spirit, not merely to appreciate human suffering but to overcome it.[15]

When we pray for what God already wants for us, we pray with his power. When we pray with the assistance of Scripture, we pray with the very words of God. The power of prayer is fully realized when we pray in the tradition of Scripture with the very Word of God. In addition to praying to God as he had revealed himself to them and using Scripture as the basis for their prayer, the early church demonstrated a humble submission to God despite their difficult circumstances.

They Submitted to God's Sovereignty

The early church did not just acknowledge God's sovereignty, but they prefaced their prayer with a tone of humble submission to it. They asked God "to do whatever [his] hand and [his] plan had predestined to take place" (Acts 4:28). They were able to look at their own circumstances through the lens of the grand story. They were not confined to the here and the now right before their eyes, but instead were able to see how their reality fit into the story God was telling. They used the truth of God's sovereignty to help them trust in God's perfect timing. God has a mysterious plan of redemption in the midst of this evil world.

How, then, should this affect our prayers? We should pray in submission to God's sovereignty and not our own perceived sovereignty. We should pray according to God's plan, trusting in his plan, not in ourselves. As the classic hymn says, "When we walk with the Lord, in the light of his word, what a glory he sheds on our way; while we do his good will, he abides with us still, and with all who will trust and obey. Trust and obey, for there's no other way to be happy in Jesus, but to trust and obey."[16] In other words, when we spend time with our Lord, it is easier to develop trust in him. What is not meant here is some kind of subjective reflection or meditation time that we spend in the

---

[15]   Kelly M. Kapic, *Embodied Hope: A Theological Meditation on Pain and Suffering* (Downers Grove, IL: IVP Academic, 2017), 84–85.

[16]   John Henry Sammis, "Trust and Obey," public domain.

presence of Jesus. While that would not be inherently bad, the point made here is more specific. When we pray in a proper manner, understanding who God has revealed himself to be while, at the same time, praying his own words back to him, we are better prepared to trust in his sovereignty over the very matters we are beseeching for. This practice, reflecting and meditating on who God is and what he is doing, removes us from our current situation and allows us to see things from God's perspective. This practice places the difficult times of our lives in their proper place: under the umbrella of an all-powerful, sovereign God who both hears and cares for us. It is then that we are moved with both our minds and hearts to obey God. The sovereignty of God and seeing the past faithfulness of the Lord ultimately moves and motivates us to pray in submission to him. When we pray for what God has already declared he wants for us, we can pray with power and confidence. When we pray with the assistance of Scripture, we pray with the very words of God. When the Lord abides with us and we with him, we pray in submission to his sovereignty. Let us now turn our attention to the heart of the early church's request in Acts 4.

They Prayed for the Lost

All the material to this point in the church's prayer was preliminary. It set the stage for the actual request. It prepared their hearts and minds and expressed their understanding of the situation before God. We can easily skip over these initial elements of prayer. It is even common to think of prayer as making requests, but that is only one aspect of prayer. Prayer, in its most basic form, is having a conversation with God. In the first few verses of the text in Acts 4, the believers converse intimately with God, but it is not until later that they share the heart of their request. So, what did they ask for?

They asked for the courage to continue to speak God's word boldly and that God would continue to reveal himself to the lost. The heart of their request was not for themselves; it was for the faithless. They wanted to see the gospel go forward: "And now, Lord, look upon their threats and grant to your servants to continue to speak your word with all boldness, while you stretch out your hand to heal, and signs and wonders are performed through the name of your holy servant Jesus" (Acts 4:29–30).

As you can see from the first part of the passage, the church sought God's help in being obedient to his call to share the gospel even amid hateful opposition. They did not rely on their own strategy or political persuasion. While the early church did strategize and lobby leaders for religious tolerance, their hope was in God's enabling power to keep them from giving in to the pressures of the world and the fears of their flesh. They wanted to be faithful to the call to share the good news about Jesus with others, and they turned to God for help. But be sure not to miss the second part of their request.

While they sought God to sustain their obedience to vocalize their faith, they also asked God to "stretch out [his] hand to heal, and [ensure] signs and wonders are performed through the name of [his] holy servant Jesus" (Acts 4:30). This request seems odd and out of place at first. Why did they pray for signs and wonders, and how did this fit with their request for God's enabling to share their faith publicly and boldly? One of the ways the truthfulness of the gospel was confirmed throughout the known world during New Testament times was through signs and wonders. In their skeptical, mystical, and polytheistic culture, God often utilized miracles or signs of various sorts to confirm the authenticity of the testimony concerning the person and work of Jesus. We see this throughout the book of Acts. Thus, the heart of their request was that they would continue to boldly share their faith and that God would continue to show the world his power through his selected prophets.

The early church wanted the world to hear, see, and believe that Jesus was the promised Messiah: he is Lord and Savior. As a result, they prayed for two primary things: their own continued faithfulness and for the lost to come to know Jesus. Are our prayers characterized by these two things? Are our typical prayer requests even in the same ballpark as these two requests? If not, why is that? It is probably because our focus is so easily removed from God and the things of God and moved to ourselves.

I (Jared) know I am so fickle. My heart is easily swayed to care about only what is best for me or what would make my own life easier or more comfortable. Thank God for continuing sanctification and the promises of his Word. Paul reminded us in Rom 8:29, "For those whom [God] foreknew he also predestined to be conformed to the image of his Son, in order that he might be the firstborn among many brothers," and in 2 Cor 3:18, "And we all, with unveiled face, beholding the glory of the Lord, are being transformed into the same image from one degree of glory to another." These are the promises to which I cling when I catch my focus turning toward myself. I look back to Christ and his Word. When we look at the cross, we tend toward faithfulness. When we look at ourselves, we tend to act in our own prideful self-interest. Then, as a by-product of selfish living, we get lost in a mire of self-hatred for not living up to our own perceived standards (which is also a form of pride). According to the example of the early church, the first thing we should pray for is our own faithfulness, specifically, faithfulness in being a witness to those around us through our words and our actions.

The second thing on that list is that the lost would come to know Jesus.

When was the last time you prayed for a specific lost person or even generally for the lost to come to know him? The apostle Paul challenged God's people to pray accordingly in 1 Tim 2:1–4, urging them to pray for those in political authority that they might be open to the church and allow the church to share the gospel freely. His reasoning in part was that God "desires all people to be saved."[17] He wrote, "First of all, then, I urge that supplications, prayers, intercessions, and thanksgivings be made for all people, for kings and all who are in high positions, that we may lead a peaceful and quiet life, godly and dignified in every way. This is good, and it is pleasing in the sight of God our Savior, who desires all people to be saved and to come to the knowledge of the truth."

In Rom 10:1, Paul further shared his heart for reaching the lost. There he highlighted his desire to see his fellow Jews come to embrace Jesus as the Messiah: "My heart's desire and prayer to God for them [Jews] is that they may be saved." Seeing the lost come to Christ should also be our hearts' desire. Our relationship with the Lord should naturally stir within us a desire to see others come to know him, and we should express this desire in prayer. Not only is it supremely good to pray that all of the lost will come to know him; we should also pray for the means by which that may happen. Jesus emphasized this aspect of prayer to his disciples when he declared, "The harvest is plentiful, but the laborers are few; therefore pray earnestly to the Lord of the harvest to send out laborers into his harvest" (Matt 9:37–38). As part of the church, we encourage you to make it a priority to pray for

- the lost generally,
- the lost people you know,
- ministers, pastors, elders,
- evangelists,
- missionaries, and
- direction on how we can go, send, or evangelize right where we are.

---

[17]   The text of 1 Tim 2:4 refers to "all" people. It seems that Paul is concerned about those in the church who would focus on one group or class of people and miss that we are called to reach all types and classes of people, which is why he encourages them to pray for kings and those in high offices. However, this view of the text does not dismiss the reality that God desires all people to repent and live in accordance with his commands. God spoke through the prophet Ezekiel and revealed, "As I live, declares the Lord GOD, I have no pleasure in the death of the wicked, but that the wicked turn from his way and live; turn back, turn back from your evil ways, for why will you die, O house of Israel?" (Ezek 33:11). Other passages affirm this truth, such as Ezek 18:23; Matt 23:37; and 2 Pet 3:9. One could even look at the Abrahamic covenant and make an argument for God's desire for all people to know him. It could be argued that the blessing of the nations is the sharing of truth to them so that they might come to embrace the truth of God and experience him as their God (Gen 12:1–3). In the end, it is right and appropriate to utilize 1 Tim 2:4 in emphasizing God's heart and desire for "all people" to be saved.

Per the early church's example, we should pray (1) Scripture to God as he has revealed himself to us, (2) in submission to his authority, (3) for our own obedience, and (4) ultimately for the salvation of the lost.

Praying Scripture

The idea of praying the Scripture deserves more attention and instruction. (As an aside, a systematized approach to prayer based on the acronym P.R.A.Y. and some corporate and personal prayer guides have been provided in the appendix.) The focus of prayer in Acts 4:24–30 is the glory of God and the advancement of the gospel. Once again, I (Jared) am struck by how different that prayer is from many of the prayers we hear and many of the prayers we ourselves utter. Observe also in this prayer how the revelation of God served as a guide and a catalyst in the early church's prayer. Some of the problems we have in our churches involve the content of our prayers. We now turn to the "how" of praying Scripture, not the overall content of prayers. We need a practical methodology for prayer and resources for prayer so that each of us might be more comfortable, more confident, and more committed to praying as the body of Christ.

The Bible can naturally serve in guiding the content of our prayers, while also serving as a catalyst for stirring our hearts to pray for other things. Many people have a unique, specialized prayer time, but you can even pray as you read the Bible. In fact, we think it is even more beneficial to pray in conjunction with your Bible reading. While reading your Bible, do so with sensitivity to the Holy Spirit prompting prayer in your heart. Allow your Bible reading to naturally flow into a time of prayer and praise of God. Our friends regularly tell us that their prayer times are not fruitful because they get easily distracted and quickly run out of content to pray. Unsure of what to pray, they allow their minds to wander, and eventually go on to do something else. From our experience, if Scripture is used as our catalyst for prayer, then we get distracted less and have plenty of content.

Specifically, Psalms provides a user-friendly and easy format for praying the Bible because the psalms were written by God for the purpose of being reflected back to God.[18] Most of the psalms are even written as prayers. At

---

[18]   Donald S. Whitney has been practicing and teaching this method for years. His book *Praying the Bible* is an excellent resource. He personally mentored me (Adam) in this method when I was his student. This section is reflective of his influence in my life. The following book may also be useful for jump-starting a practice of praying the Psalms if that is a foreign concept for you: Timothy Keller, *The Songs of Jesus: A Year of Daily Devotions in the Psalms* (New York: Viking Press, 2015).

this point, you may be saying, "Yes, I understand why you might do this, and I see why it would be helpful for me as well, but how exactly would one pray through a psalm?" Psalm 1 is a good place to begin. It reads:

> Blessed is the man who walks not in the counsel of the wicked, nor stands in the way of sinners, nor sits in the seat of scoffers; but his delight is in the law of the LORD, and on his law he meditates day and night.

> He is like a tree planted by streams of water that yields its fruit in its season, and its leaf does not wither. In all that he does, he prospers. The wicked are not so, but are like chaff that the wind drives away.

> Therefore the wicked will not stand in the judgment, nor sinners in the congregation of the righteous; for the LORD knows the way of the righteous, but the way of the wicked will perish.

To pray through this psalm, you might begin with the first part. As you read, engage the Word of God. Be sensitive to the Spirit of God stirring your heart and mind. Enter the reading with a mindset of prayer, and pray as thoughts are provoked within you from the text. For example, you read, "Blessed is the man who walks not in the counsel of the wicked, nor stands in the way of sinners, nor sits in the seat of scoffers; but his delight is in the law of the LORD, and on his law he meditates day and night" (vv. 1–2). Possibly, you feel led to begin praying for yourself: "Lord, help me to walk not in the counsel of the wicked. Instead, Lord, help me to delight in your law. Help me to love your Word. As I meditate on your Word, continue to renew my mind and change my heart." Or possibly, you find you are convicted of unconfessed sin in your life: "God, I know you desire your people to walk with you and resist the temptations of this world. I confess that I have followed the counsel of wicked people and not followed you. Lord, I confess that [mention specific sins] was sinful, and I ask for your forgiveness in Jesus. Enable me by your Spirit to be more faithful and to yield, not to temptation, but to your Spirit. Help me to walk in obedience." Or perhaps you feel led to pray for your children or spouse: "Today, Lord, my children will be bombarded with the temptation to follow the counsel of the wicked while they are at school. Help them, Lord, not to give in. Help each of them to be a wise person and submit to following your way. Help them to delight in your Word and hold fast to it as truth. Keep them from compromise, and embolden them to stand firm and live for you today." Look at all the different people and aspects of life that can be covered by those two verses alone.

Verses 3 and 4 read, "He is like a tree planted by streams of water that yields its fruit in its season, and its leaf does not wither. In all that he does, he prospers. The wicked are not so, but are like chaff that the wind drives away." Your prayer may be expressed, "Help me to yield fruit and continue to grow for your glory. Use this time with you and in your Word to produce obedience in my life. Help my spiritual life to prosper. Encourage me to walk in the Spirit and to love others well. Lead me to do justice and walk humbly."

The final two verses of Psalm 1 offer additional insights for how we should pray: "Therefore the wicked will not stand in the judgment, nor sinners in the congregation of the righteous; for the LORD knows the way of the righteous, but the way of the wicked will perish" (vv. 5–6). In response to these verses, our prayers would reflect the sentiment of the psalmist:

> Lord, please show me the way of the righteous. Draw me near to you, Lord. Use your Word to renew my mind and continually teach me to walk in righteousness. I know that the sinner and the wicked will not be able to stand in your judgment. Such would I be without the blood of Jesus Christ. God, for any of those who do not know you, I pray that they come to know you. I don't want anyone to stand before you without your declaration of righteousness and the application of your faithfulness. I specifically pray for [list lost friends] and ask you to bring them to a place of genuine faith and repentance. I also ask for the opportunity and the boldness to share the truth about Jesus with them, and that they might be receptive to his truth.

With each section, stop and pray whenever an idea is brought to your mind and heart. Continue to pray until you have said what you want to say regarding that section of the psalm or you get distracted. Then continue reading. Once prompted again, stop and pray. Continue this cycle until you run out of psalm or run out of the time you had dedicated for prayer.

We use this method in our own prayer times and have seen great improvement in those times with Jesus. A regular cycle through the book of Psalms several times a year can be organized and help to provide consistency. For example: In January, on whatever day it is, pray that psalm. For example, on January 8, pray Psalm 8. Then in February, go through the next thirty psalms. So, on February 8, pray Psalm 38. Then in March, the next thirty, and so on, until you have prayed through all the psalms. Then start over. On the thirty-first day of the month, use some part of Psalm 119. Keep in mind, the point of this system is to provide an easy method to pray faithfully to the Lord. Many of the examples we see in Scripture include speaking God's Word back to him, so we desire to be faithful by doing the same. This is only one prayer method, but we think it is a good one. Whatever method you use, we pray you will commit to being a praying member of the body of Christ.

Final Thoughts

What would it look like for you to commit to faithful prayer? It may look like

- praying through Psalms this year,
- spending time in other parts of Scripture every day, praying with fervor,
- going to a weekly prayer meeting at your local church, or
- meeting with a trusted friend to pray to the Lord together every day or once a week.

Earlier in the chapter, we wrote about Charles Spurgeon, the famed preacher. Despite Spurgeon's amazing gifts, talents, extraordinary mind, abilities, and his massive popularity, Spurgeon knew that without the power of the Spirit of God, he would be blowing hot air. He knew it took the power of the Spirit to transform lives, open eyes, convict hearts, and convert the lost. Let us not rest in our talents or our wisdom, but let us as the body of Christ come boldly before the throne of God that we might find grace to help in our time of need, recognizing that we need him every moment of every day in fulfilling his mission to make disciples. Let us pray privately as individual members of the church, and let us pray corporately together, encouraging one another in prayer.

When we pray with the assistance of Scripture, we pray with the very words of God. When we pray in submission to him, we develop further trust in him. When we pray, our focus should be his greatness while we ask God to increase our faithfulness and bring the lost to faith and repentance in Jesus Christ. So, go ahead. Pray boldly! And pray continually!

Rejoice always, pray without ceasing, give thanks in all circumstances; for this is the will of God in Christ Jesus for you. (1 Thess 5:16–18)

Personal Reflection or
Group Discussion Questions

1. Before reading this chapter, how did you think about prayer? How did you practice prayer? How about now? Has your thinking changed, and will your practice? (For those who would like further help, please use the prayer model based on the acronym P.R.A.Y. and the corporate and personal prayer guides provided in the appendix.)

2. Why is it important to address God as he has revealed himself? Meditate on some of the names of God in the Bible (Elohim, Lord, King, Jehovah-jireh, etc.). What meanings and significance do these have across the story of revelation? What meaning do they have for you in your life's story?

3. What is the importance of starting with Scripture when we pray? Have you ever been selfish in your prayers? How does Scripture help us with that? How can you begin to make Scripture the basis for your prayer time?

4. Which is more important: attitude or action? Does God care about your attitude as you come to him in prayer? Why is God's sovereignty important as a theological doctrine? As a practical matter? What does an attitude of submission look like in prayer?

5. How do you pray for your own faithfulness? How do you pray for the lost? Does the way you pray line up with the examples we see in Scripture? Do you see a change in your life when you pray for it? How can you be more intentional about praying for the lost and for those who are faithfully sharing the gospel with the lost?

6. How do you pray? What do you do in that time? Have you tried praying Scripture, and specifically Psalms? If not, what is stopping you? How can you be more intentional about prayer? How can you build Scripture into your prayer time?

Devotional

Day One: Acts 4:23–31

Have you ever prayed for boldness? What was it like? Did you receive boldness?

Open your Bible and read Acts 4:23–31.

In this passage, the believers gathered in Jerusalem to pray for boldness to proclaim the gospel.

Think deeply about the following questions:

If you have prayed for boldness, was it for selfish or unselfish reasons? These believers prayed for purely unselfish reasons. They just wanted the lost to come to know Jesus. Will you commit to praying regularly for the lost?

Pray even now for an individual you know who is not a believer.

These believers were the "goers" who went and proclaimed the gospel. If you are not a missionary, then biblically you should be a sender of missionaries. How are you contributing to the worldwide mission of reaching others for Jesus? Will you go? If not, how will you send? Will you contribute money? Will you pray for missionaries?

Pray even now for missionaries. Ask God to raise up more missionaries.

Examine the content of your prayers. Are they mostly requests? Or is there also praise and adoration? What does this say about the state of your heart?

Devotional

Day Two: Jude vv. 17–25

Do you know anyone who causes divisions and strife? What about you?

Open your Bible and read Jude vv. 17–25.

In this passage, Jude is writing to encourage believers to maintain godliness and to remember where their power comes from and how that makes them different from the world.

Think deeply about the following questions:

According to the passage, what makes believers different from the world?

The key seems to be the phrase "praying in the Holy Spirit." What does that mean?

Why and how does this make believers different from the world?

What does praying in the Holy Spirit lead to, according to the passage?

How does Jesus fit into all of this? What does he affect in this paradigm?

How should this promise drive you toward spending time with Jesus in prayer? He is the one who is truly able to keep you from stumbling.

Devotional

Day Three: Matthew 6:5–15

How would you expect Jesus to instruct us to pray?

Open your Bible and read Matthew 6:5–15.

This passage is right in the middle of the Sermon on the Mount. Jesus is presenting the values of his kingdom. He is reappropriating the law of Sinai and showing its true intent. In this specific passage, he is teaching his disciples how to pray.

Think deeply about the following questions:

Did Jesus teach his disciples to pray in the manner you expected? Explain your answer.

What does Jesus assume in the opening line of this passage? Does he command us to pray, or guide us in prayer because he assumes that we will spend time with our heavenly Father in prayer?

What can we learn from this model prayer?

Why is prayer hypocrisy denounced so harshly?

Why is it better to pray in secret and behind closed doors? Does this passage teach that one should not pray in front of other people?

What does the command to "not heap up empty phrases" mean?

The passage says, "Your kingdom come, your will be done." How does this phrase reiterate the concept of praying in light of God's sovereignty as was previously discussed in this chapter? And how should the assurance of the kingdom make us bold in prayer?

Devotional

Day Four: 1 John 5:14; Colossians 4:2; 1 Timothy 2:1–7

Do you pray in different ways? Or do you do the same old thing all the time?

Open your Bible and read 1 John 5:14; Colossians 4:2; and 1 Timothy 2:1–7.

In these passages (one written by John and two by Paul), we see that there are different kinds of prayers that are prayed by different people at different times.

Think deeply about the following questions:

What does the verse from 1 John suggest? What does that mean?

According to the verse from Colossians, how should we pray? Do you pray continually and steadfastly? What does that mean? How might that look in your own life?

Why does Paul encourage people to pray for the kings and all who are in high positions? Compare with Jer 29:7.

The Timothy passage also says something about God's desire for all people. Should that not also be our desire? How can you be intentional about praying for the lost today?

Devotional

Day Five: John 17:6–26

Did you know Jesus prayed for you before he was crucified? What would you have wanted him to pray on your behalf?

Open your Bible and read John 17:6–26.

In this passage, we see that before Jesus was crucified, he prayed for the church.

Think deeply about the following questions:

This prayer is known as the High Priestly Prayer. Why do you think it is called that? Read Heb 4:14–11:39 for further clarification, focusing in on 4:14–5:10 and 8:1–9:14.

What was the purpose of this prayer?

Jesus is clearly very concerned about his present and future followers. In what similar ways can we legitimately pray for the church?

How can we plan to pray as Jesus did?

CHAPTER 4

GIVING CHURCH:
We Consider Others

Radical generosity was a central characteristic of the early church, as detailed in the book of Acts.

> And they devoted themselves to the apostles' teaching and the fellowship, to the breaking of bread and the prayers. And awe came upon every soul, and many wonders and signs were being done through the apostles. *And all who believed were together and had all things in common. And they were selling their possessions and belongings and distributing the proceeds to all, as any had need.* And day by day, attending the temple together and breaking bread in their homes, they received their food with glad and generous hearts, praising God and having favor with all the people. And the Lord added to their number day by day those who were being saved. (Acts 2:42–47)

Unique Provisions through Sensitive Servants

On March 17, 1993, arsonists burned down Springhill Baptist Church, just outside of Springfield, Missouri. Springhill was a small rural church, yet in the wake of that disaster, its members believed God had called them as a church to impact their world with the gospel. They cried, they prayed, and they continued to serve by faith despite having lost their building. Consequently, they saw God move in amazing ways. God provided uniquely for the church and revealed himself to the congregation during the rebuilding process. God provided land through the generosity of another congregation. People rallied, and money seemed to arrive just in time. Members described several roadblocks they faced as they were rebuilding, and they did not know how they would move forward. For example, they desperately needed Sheetrock work performed, but they could not afford to hire anyone, so they prayed. Then, something amazing happened.

One day, while congregants were working on the building, a truckload of men pulled up. They got out of their truck and said they had heard about the fire on the news. The men, all from Texas, explained that God had told them to come up and help. Apologetically, they said that they did not know how much help they would be . . . the only thing they really knew how to do was hang Sheetrock!

Another time, the church needed $500 to pay for some construction work. They prayed and believed God for the money. That week, a man drove up to the rebuild site and said the Lord had led him to give some money to help the rebuilding effort. He handed them $500.[1]

While many more amazing stories could be told highlighting the faith and faithfulness of God's people, notice in the events I just described how believers gave generously and sacrificially of their time, their abilities, and their finances. The people of God sacrificed for the good of the kingdom. Things did not just appear. Springhill did not just pray, walk into the building, and see Sheetrock on the walls. No, God sent people to do the work. God sent money to pay for it. God was in control, but he used the generosity of his people to accomplish his goals.

This was the Lord's method in Acts as well. The church gave generously of themselves and their possessions for the good of the kingdom. They experienced great suffering and persecution. As a result, believers were scattered throughout the known world, yet they continued to give generously. At one point, Christians in Antioch sent money back to the home church in Jerusalem to help support her (Acts 11:29–30). God's church has always been characterized by radical generosity. That same mark of generosity that

---

[1]   Charles Dixon and Carl Holman, who were present and part of the rebuilding effort, related these stories personally to me (Adam) around March 2015.

was evident in the early church, that was evident in the believers who came to Springhill's aid, should also be evident in our lives today, both as we meet collectively as the church and as we live individually as believers in Jesus. God wants to reveal himself through you as you give generously of yourself and your possessions for his glorious purposes.

A Sober Realization

For years, I (Adam) remember striving to promote myself, to be someone, to be remembered by others and thought of as important. This desire to be known, remembered, and respected by others drove me in some unhealthy ways. I even remember telling someone in my high school, "One day, I'm going to be in the newspaper." Well, one day, I was featured in the newspaper. That day came and went, and it did not satisfy. I dreamed of being wealthy. Then one day, I was confronted by the wisdom of the preacher of Ecclesiastes: "I hated all my toil in which I toil under the sun, seeing that I must leave it to the man who will come after me, and who knows whether he will be wise or a fool? Yet he will be master of all for which I toiled and used my wisdom under the sun. This also is vanity" (Eccl 2:18–19). I realized that in the end I will likely die with money that I never got to enjoy. I realized that the money I save and amass will just be divided up and given to others. Furthermore, I remember reading and realizing that the accumulation of wealth would not satisfy the longings of my soul. A cool car was also on my list. Well, I ended up getting one, and then I found myself wanting a better car. I remember wanting to be a man with the privileges and responsibility of manhood. I became a man, and then I wanted to be a kid again. I came to the sober realization that when life's pursuits are centered on me, they do not satisfy.

As the Lord worked in my life through the Bible's teaching and the presence of his Spirit, my perspective began to shift. God slowly crafted a new set of lenses through which I could see. Through that process, some questions developed that have since helped shape the course of my life and the decisions I make. Here are three of them.

1. *Who has made the biggest positive impact on my life?*
   I have concluded that the people who have the biggest impact on my life are those who loved me and invested in me. What about you? Who has impacted your life for the better? Asking this question is helpful

because it reminds me that the things that matter in life are not material but personal. What if you cannot think of someone who has impacted you in this way? This can be even greater motivation for you moving forward. The things that truly matter in life are personal, and you have the opportunity to make an impact in others' lives in ways that you may not yet have experienced.

2. *Is life about me or someone bigger than me?*
   Life is about so much more than me. Part of that truth has been shaped by the fact that I now have a family, but another, deeper part of that truth has been developed because I have come to realize that in salvation God has called all of us. He has given us a purpose and a plan. He wants to be glorified in our lives. He wants to use our lives to draw others into a relationship with him. He wants to use all of us and has a specific purpose for you. The Great Commission of Matt 28:19–20 applies to all who believe in Jesus Christ.

3. *Is God calling me to store up or sell out?*
   A professor in Bible college once emphasized this important reality: "God doesn't give you more so that you can spend more. God gives you more so that you can give more." God calls us to so much more than simply storing up and hoarding for the future. He is calling us to give of ourselves out of what we have for the good of others and for the good of God's people. That is how he has called his church to live.

Storing Up or Selling Out?

Throughout Acts, we can see what the church of God is meant to be and find generosity to be a central characteristic. In Acts 2:42–47, the church models God's intention for his people. They are a giving church. They gave generously of their possessions, homes, food, finances, time, abilities, and more. Their generous attitude and giving heart are seen also in Acts 4:32–36.

> Now the full number of those who believed were of one heart and soul, and no one said that any of the things that belonged to him was his own, but they had everything in common. And with great power the apostles were giving their testimony to the resurrection of the Lord Jesus, and great grace was upon them all. There was not a

' needy person among them, for as many as were owners of lands or houses sold them and brought the proceeds of what was sold and laid it at the apostles' feet, and it was distributed to each as any had need.

Not one of the church members had need of anything. They were constantly generous and giving toward one another, and more converts were being added every day.

This passage explicitly talks about sharing wealth within the church to help other members. To many, this notion may sound strangely un-American and anti-capitalist, but it is assuredly biblical. While this may be true, it is important not to jump to any hasty conclusions. This passage is certainly not describing a form of government or oversight of an economic system as some would seek to suggest. Instead, it is describing the heart of Christians for others. It is showing the collective characterization of people who have been transformed by a God who generously extended his grace to them. Christians are willing to give up what they have for the sake of others because Christ gave up his life for them. Just as this attitude was the heart of the early disciples, so too should this be the heart of modern Christians.

In Acts 5:1–11, we read of a situation that arose, which was contrary to God's vision for the church. Within this situation, we see manipulation, deceit, selfishness, self-promotion, and a lack of generosity. Ananias and Sapphira were members of the early church. Together, they willingly sold some property and gave some of the proceeds to the church. There is no indication in the text that they were required to sell the property. There is no indication that they were required to give any of the proceeds to the church, yet they did both. Despite the goodness of their actions, a problem was revealed. While they claimed to have given all of the profit, they actually kept some back for themselves. Luke does not disclose why they did this, but it seems that they wanted to keep up appearances and pretend to be sacrificing to the same extent as others. Such pretense goes against the attitude God desires for his people and their generosity. We are called to be generous because of the mission of God, not the preservation and promotion of self.

We Should Steward as Generous Givers

God calls his church to sell out, not store up. Such sacrificial generosity is not just in relation to our finances, but with all that God has entrusted to us. In

Matthew 25, Jesus tells a story commonly known as the parable of the talents.[2] In this story, a master gives three of his servants different amounts of money before going on a long trip. He gives one servant one talent, another two talents, and to the third, five talents. When the master returns, he finds that the two servants who had been given multiple talents had worked to multiply the master's money even further, but the servant with only one talent still had only one talent. The good servants are subsequently rewarded, and the wicked servant is punished. This story has much to teach us. Like the master, God entrusts all people to be good stewards of all that he gives them. We are to put what God has given us to work for him. Like the two good servants, God's people will be rewarded when they diligently serve God. Our motivation for working for the kingdom of God is first that God loved us and second that we now desire to do good as well. Like the wicked servant, those who do not serve him will be punished with separation from God. This parable speaks of the master giving his servants money. What does God, our Master, give to us to steward well? There are five commodities of life God has given us to steward for his glory. As we steward these, we, as the church, are to do so with the same attitude of generosity demonstrated in the book of Acts.

Treasures

The first commodity God has called believers to steward generously is their finances and possessions. This component is the most obvious one and the one we tend to think of immediately when the topic of giving comes up. It should come as no real surprise that we should give generously of our money. The passages from Acts provided earlier in this chapter demonstrate the early church's financial generosity. They gave of their money, land, and homes for the sake of others. We should desire to use the money and possessions we treasure for the sake of the kingdom. Just think: how much of our money is spent on excessive food, eating out, energy drinks, movies, cable TV, lawn maintenance, gaming, mobile phones, and so forth? Many other items could be added to this list. How much of our money is spent on things that do not last? How much of our money is spent on our own pleasure, without thought of others? Think about that in contrast with how much of our money is leveraged for the kingdom of God. If we have been given the riches of grace, should we not respond accordingly with the riches within our care?

A story has been told about a six-year-old kid named Steve who would

---

[2]   Feel free to put this book down and go read Matt 25:14–30 before continuing, as we will be providing merely a summary of this important passage.

sometimes go with his pastor-dad to the Thursday morning Bible study. At the Bible study, an elderly man named George would always split his donut with Steve. One Sunday, Steve came to church with a sandwich bag full of Cheerios. George leaned over and asked Steve if he could have some. Steve reached in his bag, pulled out a Cheerio, and split it in half, giving George half a Cheerio. While we may not say it or even think it, our practical view of generosity is often like Steve's. God gives us so much, and we so often give him back half a Cheerio.[3]

What answers would arise if we honestly asked ourselves the types of questions listed earlier? How often do I reason my way out of being generous? How often do I find something "better" to use my money for? What if your child came to you and said, "I believe God is calling me to give my college savings to the poor and work my way through school"? What would you say? Would you trust God in that moment? I think most of us would argue and debate about the practical implications. We might press her to question whether she is truly hearing from God. We might challenge her motives and seek to cast doubt on such an "irresponsible" decision. Ultimately, most of us would probably try to talk her out of being so generous. Now, to be fair, that is an extreme example, but if we are honest, we regularly reason our way out of being generous people. What do you do when you see a homeless person and feel led to give? Some of us say no because we assume and reason, "They will just go and buy liquor and drugs." How do we know, and when did God hold us responsible for someone else's use of the funds we give? Years ago, I was helping a homeless woman when I distinctly felt led to give her my coat. I resisted because I really liked my coat. I debated about giving her money, and various other things. In the end, I took so long reasoning within myself that it was now awkward, the moment was gone, and so was she. Can you imagine? I felt led to give her my jacket, yet I reasoned myself out of being obedient.

Paul speaks of this very issue to the Corinthians: "The point is this: whoever sows sparingly will also reap sparingly, and whoever sows bountifully will also reap bountifully. Each one must give as he has decided in his heart, not reluctantly or under compulsion, for God loves a cheerful giver. And God is able to make all grace abound to you, so that having all sufficiency in all things at all times, you may abound in every good work" (2 Cor 9:6–8). Here Paul is saying that what is given for the kingdom's sake will be reaped mightily for the kingdom. We are called to sell out, not store up. All the while, our

---

[3]   Lou Nicholes, "Giving Half a Cheerio," Family Times website, accessed January 23, 2019, https://www.family-times.net/illustration/Generosity/201182/.

motive for doing so is one of cheer and not fear. We give to the kingdom because we love God and desire his kingdom to be made known, not out of some vague sense of duty or need to earn some standing. We have been given so much that we should desire to give out of love.

To get some perspective regarding the stewarding of our treasures, consider asking yourself these questions: Do I give faithfully and sacrificially to my local church? Do I pray about how I use my resources? Do I seek wisdom in how to use my car, land, investments, and home for the sake of others and their needs? Or, do I solely seek to leverage these things for my good and the good of my family?

Using our resources for the work of the Lord comes with certain sacrifices. For example, if you open up your home to minister to others, you should expect spills, breaks, dents, and scratches. Just the other day, my wife and I (Adam) were hosting a middle school small group in our home. One boy tromped off our sidewalk through the mud, into our house, and down our stairs, leaving muddy prints in our carpet. Ministry is messy! But we are called to love others, and we are called to use our treasures for the sake of others. This text in Acts indeed emphasized financial generosity, but the church was exceedingly generous in other ways as well.

Time

Time is the second valuable commodity the Lord has given the church to steward. This commodity is slightly less obvious than treasure, but I think most of us still think about our time as a resource to be used well. In Acts, we see the church giving of their time by gathering, encouraging, giving to the poor, discussing theology and ministry, engaging at the temple, and overall leveraging resources for the sake of others. Each of these things took time, time they could have used doing something else or nothing at all. Each of these things required a sacrifice of time. However, they saw the mission of the church as more important than their personal preferences and schedules. The author of Hebrews makes sure his people consider their time and how it is spent: "Do not neglect to do good and to share what you have, for such sacrifices are pleasing to God" (Heb 13:16). We ought to be doing good and sharing with others, not just our resources, but also our time. And do not forget: our motivation for this giving is not duty, but delight. We love the Lord our God. We have first been loved by the Lord Jesus, and now we give cheerfully to others out of what we have been given. How much of our time is spent on things that do not last? How much of our time is leveraged for the kingdom of God?

It could be that there are opportunities all around us, beckoning us to consider blessing others with our time. We all have time to give. Honestly process some of these questions and your answers: What am I doing with my time that is so valuable? Why can't I serve with my church? Why can't I invite my neighbors over for dinner to get to know them and invest in their lives? Why can't I babysit for free for the couple in the apartment across the hall and give them a well-needed break? Why can't I serve at the local women's shelter? Why can't I cook a meal for the new family at church? Maybe there are other types of questions you could ask, but hopefully this gets your thoughts rolling in the right direction. Do I consider others more important than myself? Are others worth the giving up of my downtime? Am I willing to be inconvenienced? We as Christians are called to use our time to love and serve others. If we are honest, our time feels restricted and limited because we are pursuing entertainment, pleasure, sports, or money and not the kingdom of God.

Now, as an aside, this section is not advocating that each of us stay constantly busy in the work of the Lord or that we run ourselves and our families ragged. Burnout is real, and life balance is important. This section is not advocating that you try to do everything and help everyone. That is not it. The goal is to see that the church in Acts stewarded and sacrificed of their time for the sake of others in doing the work of the Lord. And the logical question is, Am I? Are you? Are we as the church? Are we challenging one another to be generous with our time?

Talents

God has also given us talents (special abilities) to steward, and he has called his church to be generous in using their talents for the building up of others and the promotion of his kingdom. The early church in Acts gave of their talents for the sake of the church and for the sake of others. We see them giving of their abilities in hospitality, preaching, healings, management, and more. The apostles faithfully studied and taught. Others opened up their homes for the church to gather. Others performed signs and wonders. Others managed the distribution of the gifts given by the church to get the appropriate material to those in need. We see this reality throughout Acts, but it's possibly most evident in Acts 6 with seven men who were selected to manage the feeding of neglected widows in a fair manner.

Just as the early church used the abilities they were given for the body of Christ, so should we. Each of us as members of the church has been given gifts by the Spirit of God for the edification of the body. Paul wrote:

For by the grace given to me I say to everyone among you not to think of himself more highly than he ought to think, but to think with sober judgment, each according to the measure of faith that God has assigned. For as in one body we have many members, and the members do not all have the same function, so we, though many, are one body in Christ, and individually members one of another. Having gifts that differ according to the grace given to us, let us use them: if prophecy, in proportion to our faith; if service, in our serving; the one who teaches, in his teaching; the one who exhorts, in his exhortation; the one who contributes, in generosity; the one who leads, with zeal; the one who does acts of mercy, with cheerfulness. (Rom 12:3–8)[4]

We are called by God to serve in accordance with the giftedness we have received from God. Not to do so would be selfish on our part and rebellion against God's design and desire.

How can you and I become more aware of our talents and commit more diligently to use them for the Lord? What if we sat down and processed these types of questions? Do I ever ask others what passions or gifts for the Lord they see in my life? If so, what do they tell me? What gifting or passion do I see in myself? Am I serving the Lord by using these passions and abilities, these gifts? Am I willing to serve where I am needed or only where I want? These questions are good gauges for where we may be spiritually on this issue. Just as the church in Acts was called, so too are we called to give of our talents for the kingdom.

Temple

The fourth commodity we, as the church, are called to steward is our own physical bodies. The Bible reveals that when we place our faith in Jesus and become believers, God places his Spirit in us. We each become a living temple of God. As Paul reminded the Corinthians, "Or do you not know that your body is a temple of the Holy Spirit within you, whom you have from God? You are not your own, for you were bought with a price. So glorify God in your body" (1 Cor 6:19–20).

In Acts, the early church sacrificed their bodies and their very lives for the sake of the gospel of Jesus Christ. Paul spoke of giving your whole life as a living sacrifice for the Lord (Rom 12:1–2). By this he meant living our lives in the service of the Lord. Our lives belong to Jesus. We are to offer ourselves to him to be used by him for the promotion of his glory and his kingdom.

---

4   See also 1 Cor 12.1–30; Eph 4:7–16; 1 Pet 4:10–11.

One great, but extreme, example is found in Acts 7. In this passage, Stephen becomes the church's first martyr. He literally gave his life for the sake of the gospel. Up until now, we have been talking about ways we are called to be generous in certain areas of our lives. Here we begin to see the full picture: we are called to serve and love generously in all areas of our lives. In fact, our lives should be characterized by this full devotion.

Think about the idea of salvation as signing the rights of your life over to Jesus. Your life belongs to him, and you are commissioned to live for him. Your body belongs to him. With this idea in mind, reflect on these questions: Am I more worried about dying or living well? Does staying alive and comfortable motivate me or does living and loving others well motivate me? Am I using my body in service of the Lord? Is there risk involved in the way I serve God and love others? If not, it may be a sign that your own comfort motivates you more than God's calling. Ministry is risky, after all. Risk is right.[5] Even more pointedly, ask yourself these questions: Do I think about how I eat and how my energy, health, and diet can impact how God can use me? Do I ensure my body gets proper sleep on Saturday night in preparation for Sunday ministry? These types of questions help reveal the values and commitments of our hearts. Just as the early church committed their bodies to the Lord, so should we.

Testimony

The final commodity we are given to steward is our testimonies. What is a testimony? Primarily, a "testimony" is the story of how God has worked in your life. Your testimony is your "God story."

The church was called to make disciples by inviting others to follow Jesus as part of their community (Acts 1:8). They called others to acknowledge that Jesus was the Messiah. He was the one who delivered all who would believe in him from bondage and spiritual death. It was he who atoned for sin. He gave meaning to life. He was the only one worthy of their lives and devotion, because he alone secured a future kingdom for them, a kingdom that could not be denied by the temporary rulers of this age. So, the early church shared how God had worked in their lives both individually and collectively, in the life of the church. They shared about their experiences with Jesus. In other words, they shared their *testimonies*.

The book of Acts details the lives of Peter and Paul as a testimony of Christ's transformative work. Peter specifically leveraged the testimony of Old

---

[5]   As John Piper wrote in Piper, *Risk Is Right: Better to Risk Your Life Than to Waste It* (Wheaton, IL: Crossway, 2013), 17.

Testament saints and his own witness of the crucifixion and resurrection of Jesus in Acts 3:12–16.[6] Peter and John even went so far as to declare that their experience with Jesus compelled them to speak about him. They testified that they could not be silent, but must speak about what they had seen and heard of Jesus (Acts 4:19–20). They, along with the other apostles, continued to give "testimony to the resurrection of the Lord Jesus," both to encourage other believers and to inform those ignorant of the person and work of Jesus (Acts 4:33). Their personal experience was a foundation for validating their witness to others again in Acts 5:32. It was Peter's personal testimony of the conversion of the Gentile Cornelius that convinced the early church that Gentiles could be saved just as Jews were (Acts 11:1–18). Peter's instructions, supplemented by Paul and Barnabas, reinforced this reality with the leaders of the church in Acts 15:1–12. When Paul spoke to the hostile mob around him in Jerusalem, he shared his personal testimony regarding his encounter with Jesus (Acts 22:3–21).

All who are born again have had a personal encounter with Jesus. Your personal experience is a powerful platform God has given to you. Your story does not have to be dramatic. You do not have to exaggerate your sinfulness before coming to Jesus or the details around coming to Jesus. You just need to share your personal story with honesty and humility. Our part is to share what God has done in our lives. God's part is to use that testimony in the lives of the hearer.

Has God done something in your life? If you are a Christian, then of course God has done something in your life! He has done a miracle in you. He brought you from death to life. That is amazing. That is a testimony. We all have a responsibility to generously share our testimonies with others. Sharing our stories glorifies God while informing and encouraging others concerning how God works and how one is saved. Some of us may think that others have "exciting" testimonies compared to our "boring" ones, but this is a lie. If we have indeed encountered the God of the universe and we have been made spiritually alive by him, then we each have a powerful testimony regarding the miracle of grace. Who needs to hear your story? The world and church alike benefit from hearing our testimonies. The church benefits by way of encouragement. The world benefits because it can serve as motivation for belief. The Lord can use the stories of our changed lives to change someone else's life. Share with others what God has done and is doing in your life.

One Sunday before our church service began, a man requested to speak privately with me (Adam). He asked me if I remembered my sermon from the previous week. I smiled. Yes. He went on to recount details from the sermon.

---

6   See also Acts 10:34–43.

He talked about the Christian's responsibility to share God's truth, specifically regarding salvation, with others. He remembered my suggestion, that an easy way to talk to people about God is to relate one's own experience with God. Most people will listen politely and engage in that conversation. He had never shared his faith with anyone, and the thought of doing so was terrifying. Nevertheless, he was convinced from Scripture that he could and should do this. So, that week at work, he began to share his testimony with a coworker. He said it was amazing. It opened up all types of conversation and questions. In the end, he had an opportunity to pray with that coworker. While the coworker did not immediately surrender his life to Jesus, he was open to further conversations and even interested in exploring the claims of Christ.

Now, do all testimony encounters have happy endings? No, they do not. You may encounter someone ready to surrender to Jesus. Then again, you may be ridiculed. You will get reactions all along that spectrum. In any case, will you be faithful to share with others what God has done and is doing in your life? Will you be a witness of who God is and what he has done for all humankind?

One way to be faithful with this witness is to realize that your testimony (the story of how God has called you to him) is the gospel in miniature. In recounting how God restored our relationship with him, we have a great opportunity to point to the bigger story of how God is restoring all of creation. In 2 Timothy 1, Paul, writing to his protégé Timothy, says, "I am reminded of your sincere faith, a faith that dwelt first in your grandmother Lois and your mother Eunice and now, I am sure, dwells in you as well. For this reason I remind you to fan into flame the gift of God, which is in you through the laying on of my hands" (vv. 5–7). Paul is encouraging Timothy to steward well the good deposit of the gospel that his faithful family had passed to him. That is our calling as well, as believers. We must steward the gospel well. How does one do that? By sharing it with others, by sowing the seeds of the gospel so that they can be watered and grow again. Paul adds, "Therefore do not be ashamed of the testimony about our Lord" (v. 8). We must not be ashamed of Jesus, of the stories of our own conversion, or of our hope for the restoration of all things.

Here are some final questions to ask yourself: Am I engaging the world with my testimony? How often do I have conversations with others in which I could talk about my relationship with God? Am I willing to have such conversations with others when the opportunity arises? Do I pray for opportunities? Do I pray for the courage and clarity to share my testimony? We are called as Christians to be generous with our testimonies because we all have a story about how Jesus has impacted our lives.

Final Thoughts

A couple of years ago, some friends gave our family (Adam's) a terrific thirteen-by-thirteen-foot trampoline. Their children had gotten older, and they did not want it anymore. A couple of weeks after we assembled it in our backyard, some of my children asked me to help them learn how to do a backflip. The first thing I did was show them a backflip so they would see how it was done. Then I told them to try.

They would start well. They would bounce really high. But then, just as they started the flip, they would get scared, twist around and bail out of the flip, and land on their knees. I repeatedly told them, "You have to quit worrying about whether you are going to get hurt or what might go wrong. Instead, you have to focus on what you are going to do and commit to doing it. You have to commit. You have to sell out." I explained, "If you are focused on what can go wrong, if you let fear and anxiety control you, you will not complete the flip; but if you commit and sell out, you can do it."

God has called his church to sell out, not store up. He has called us to commit and to see ourselves as a means for reaching others. To sell out, we have to refocus on God and the truth of his Word and not focus on our fears, our anxieties, and what can go wrong. Well-known pastor and author Francis Chan described Christianity this way: "Becoming a Christian is a complete and total surrender of your own desires and flesh to the higher purpose of serving God's glory."[7] We must be careful not to let fear and selfishness keep us from surrendering our desires and being the generous people God has called us to be.

A friend of mine and one of the most giving people I have ever met has this well-used quote at the bottom of his emails:

> Life is not a journey to the grave with the intention of arriving in a pretty and well-preserved body, but rather to skid in broadside, thoroughly used up, totally worn out, and loudly proclaiming . . . "Wow, what a ride!"[8]

Why does my friend use this quote? Because he understood a long time ago that God has called his church to sell out, not store up. He calls his church to be a *giving* church. The early church understood, believed, and practiced this truth. The question is, do we?

---

[7]   Francis Chan, *Letters to the Church* (Colorado Springs: David C. Cook, 2018), 130.
[8]   Various versions of this popular quote exist as a quote by Hunter Thompson.

Personal Reflection or
Group Discussion Questions

1. Before reading this chapter, how did you think about giving in the context of the church? Has this chapter impacted the way you see giving?

2. What is your life about? If someone looked at how you spend your money, would your checkbook point to the same answer? What are other treasures you possess other than money that you could leverage for the kingdom of God?

3. How could you steward your resources to better demonstrate God's purpose for your life?

4. Do you regularly use your time to encourage and build up other believers? How is your time usually spent?

5. What talents do you possess? Do you regularly use your talents for the sake of others? Are there talents you have that you could leverage but have never thought could benefit others?

6. With whom have you recently shared your testimony? Is there an unsaved friend who came to mind as you read? If so, your story could be used by God to spark belief. Is there someone in your local church who could benefit from hearing about how God has been faithful in your life?

Devotional

Day One: Acts 2:42–47

Have you ever fallen on hard times and had a good friend bail you out? How did that feel? Have you ever provided for someone else when that person was in need? How did that person react?

Open your Bible and read Acts 2:42–47.

In this passage, Luke, the author of the book of Acts, described how the new Christian community (the church) was functioning and the spirit and attitude that characterized it. We have looked at this passage before, but here it will be with a different emphasis.

Think deeply about the following questions:

What does it mean that "all who believed were together and had all things in common"? Does anything you see in your church context or in your own life even come close to resembling what is described here?

The passage next says that "they were selling their possessions and belongings and distributing the proceeds to all, as any had need." What does this suggest about the believers? What (or whom) did they care about most?

How does this passage challenge our understanding of giving in the church?

Would you be willing to sell a car to see someone else's needs met? What about a TV or gaming system? Would you even consider giving to the church (or simply someone in need in the body of Christ) an amount larger than your typical monthly tithe?

How does this passage motivate you to give more freely of your treasure, time, talent, temple, or testimony?

Devotional

Day Two: Acts 4:32–36

Have you ever experienced true, deep, and abiding community? What would a community like that be like?

Open your Bible and read Acts 4:32–36.

In this passage, we see again the heart of the early church for one another, especially regarding money and financial need.

Think deeply about the following questions:

Yesterday's devotional dealt primarily with the text's emphasis on financial giving. How does this text speak to the other areas of giving discussed in this chapter (time, talents, temple, and testimony)?

What guidance do the apostles and the model of the early church give us for evaluating our generosity in all areas of our lives?

How can you leverage your free time better for the sake of the body of Christ?

How can you leverage your temple for the kingdom?

How can your talents and testimony be helpful to the kingdom of God?

Commit to implementing one of these ideas today.

Devotional

Day Three: Acts 5:1–11

If you answered no to yesterday's first question and have never experienced true, deep, abiding community, then would it surprise you that it is God's intention for you to have such an experience? In fact, it seems from Scripture that when his church is not participating in and fostering this kind of community, it is in sin.

Open your Bible and read Acts 5:1–11.

In this passage, we see God punish Ananias and Sapphira for lying to the Holy Spirit and for acting out of self-interest instead of focusing on the best interest of the whole community of believers. The fact that God punished them shows us that they sinned.

Think deeply about the following questions:

How have you acted out of self-interest in the past when God was calling you to focus on others?

Are there ways you are actively sinning that could affect your brothers and sisters in Christ?

What decisions do you have to make in the coming days, weeks, and months that could affect others in the body of Christ?

How is this way of thinking different from the world's way of thinking?

Is there something concrete you can do this week with your treasure, time, talents, temple, or testimony to glorify God and build up his church?

Devotional

Day Four: Romans 12:1–8

Have you ever seen an animal slaughtered? Our modern sensibilities recoil from such a suggestion in disgust, but the biblical world is filled with sacrifices and sacrificial imagery.

Open your Bible and read Romans 12:1–8.

In this passage, Paul tells Christians that we are to present our lives as sacrifices to God, and then Paul immediately describes the unity of the body of Christ.

Think deeply about the following questions:

What does it mean that our lives are to be "living sacrifices"? How can a sacrifice be living?

What does presenting your body as a living sacrifice have to do with living a generous life as a believer?

Why does Paul talk about unity in the body of Christ immediately after describing the Christian life as a living sacrifice? How would offering your life as a living sacrifice affect the body of Christ?

How do you live a sacrificial life for the sake of others? What do you give up for the sake of others? How do you daily live out this biblical command? Weekly? Yearly?

How can you use your specific God-given gifts to do this?

Recognizing that all our service is empowered by the Holy Spirit, how can you give and serve more effectively this week?

Devotional

Day Five: Ephesians 4:1–16

How does unity tie into being generous? How are the two attitudes related?

Open your Bible and read Ephesians 4:1–16.

In this passage, Paul discussed the worthy way that Christians are called to live. A large part of living as a Christian involves living in unity with the body of Christ.

Think deeply about the following questions:

How does living in unity with the rest of the body of Christ entail giving? What is the connection?

You have a unique part to play in the body of Christ. What are your talents? How can you steward them for the sake of the whole body of Christ?

To be unified (that is, to "maintain the unity of the Spirit in the bond of peace"), we have to "[bear] with one another in love." What does this mean? What are some practical ways to do this?

In the midst of unity and striving to stay unified, we must remember that we are all on the same level. We have all been shown grace and mercy at the foot of the cross. Why do we need to remember this? How should God's grace inform our interactions with others?

How does this passage motivate you to give more freely of your treasure, time, talent, temple, or testimony?

CHAPTER 5

ENGAGING CHURCH:
We Pursue the Lost

Cultural engagement for the sake of the gospel was a central characteristic of the early church as detailed in the book of Acts.

> And they devoted themselves to the apostles' teaching and the fellowship, to the breaking of bread and the prayers. And awe came upon every soul, and many wonders and signs were being done through the apostles. And all who believed were together and had all things in common. And they were selling their possessions and belongings and distributing the proceeds to all, as any had need. *And day by day, attending the temple together* and breaking bread in their homes, they received their food with glad and generous hearts, praising God and having favor with all the people. *And the Lord added to their number day by day those who were being saved.* (Acts 2:42–47)

Process Needed

Nine years into our marriage, our family was growing faster than our resources. Consequently, we had to put multiple kids in one room. For those who are

99

unfamiliar with our story, Adrienne and I (Adam) went from not being able to have kids to not being able *not* to have kids. It was crazy, terrifying, and exciting all at the same time. To maximize space, we decided to get a bunk bed for our two oldest daughters to share a room. My wife looked around and purchased a good, affordable bunk bed for them. When I say she bought a bunk bed, what I mean is she bought bunk bed parts that needed assembly.

I opened the box and pieces went everywhere. It was ridiculous. Nothing was preassembled. Every piece of that thing was detached from every other piece. I breathed deeply and dove in. I separated the pieces, but I did not see the instructions. Where were they? I looked all over the floor. They were not there. Since we had dumped the box, I assumed they had fallen out, but maybe they were stuck inside. Sure enough, they were. Well, not "they," but "it." To call it "instructions" is overly generous: it was a one-page diagram, with each part *near* its adjoining part, and an arrow pointing. One page, one image. No steps. No written direction. Just an incomplete picture with an assumption that I had an engineering degree. I had the plan (to put the bed together), but the problem was that I was missing the process (a system for how to do it).

Many people in the church can relate. They have the plan (to make disciples), but they have no idea really where to begin. They are missing a process for reaching and ministering to others. They feel stuck, lost, and ill-equipped for the task at hand. Many never try. Some do, but get frustrated. A few muddle their way through and end up eventually figuring it out.

This chapter is designed to help. The early church in Acts had a simple process they followed for making disciples. This process flowed from one word: *engagement*. The word *engaging* describes the outreach of the church. We tend to think of disciple-making (evangelism/spiritual growth) as a program or as something awkward and unnatural, but it does not have to be. In fact, the biblical ideal is that evangelism and the resulting maturation of faith are natural and organic. Acts provides a helpful model for how the early church engaged the culture around them. Some of these engagement encounters seem more planned, while others happened as opportunities spontaneously arose in the course of everyday events.

Before moving into the engagement process, it is important to acknowledge that while this chapter is last, it is truly foundational to all the early church did. Acts 1:8 is the theme verse for the book of Acts: "But you will receive power when the Holy Spirit has come upon you, and you will be my witnesses in Jerusalem and in all Judea and Samaria, and to the end of the earth." Every Spirit-baptism episode (Acts 2, 8, 10, 19) is an unfolding of Acts 1:8, showing

God's fulfillment in sending Spirit-empowered gospel witnesses to the end of the known world.[1] The early church was empowered by the Spirit, in part, to engage its culture with the gospel; and just as that was part of the Spirit's purpose in the community's life as a church, so it is our purpose still today.

Planned Engagement

Acts 2:46–47

Luke recounted multiple instances of planned or intentional engagement in the book of Acts. In Acts 2:46–47, he says, "And day by day, attending the temple together and breaking bread in their homes, they received their food with glad and generous hearts, praising God and having favor with all the people. And the Lord added to their number day by day those who were being saved." We have read this passage many times over the course of this book, but let us slow down here and dive a little deeper into these particular verses. This point is subtle in the text, but significant when studied in depth. Notice that these new Christians were still going to the temple. Why? After all, they were no longer worshiping through the priest and the temple. They had come to accept Jesus as their sacrifice and high priest who provided them with direct access before the throne of almighty God (see Heb 4:14–16; 10:1–22). The veil of the temple had been torn signifying that all now had direct access to God through Jesus (Matt 27:51). So why were they still attending a place that did not reflect their new reality of worship? Because that was where people were. It was where people looking for God were, where people stuck in religious traditions were. The temple was where the markets were. It was the place where people sold goods and sought answers. The temple of Jerusalem was the hub of the city, and those nearest it were primed for spiritual conversation.

The early church was still going to the temple (and later to the synagogues) to engage people where they were. They leveraged this location and the events surrounding it to engage people with the good news of Jesus Christ. They took advantage of the opportunity they had to speak about Jesus and share the new hope they had.

Dig down a little further in this text. See another subtle statement that helps qualify their cultural engagements. Pay careful attention to the description

---

[1]   For more on the role of Acts 1:8 and the Spirit-baptism episodes in Acts, see P. Adam McClendon, *Paul's Spirituality in Galatians: A Critique of Contemporary Spiritualities* (Eugene, OR: Wipf & Stock, 2015), 59–65.

of their relationships. These new believers had "favor with all the people" (Acts 2:47). Relationship and respect were present in their approach and encounters. These believers lived in a manner consistent with the faith they professed. They also approached and engaged people in a way that demonstrated an authentic care for them. Their engagement was not for the purpose of growing a big gathering, but for seeing people repent and come to faith in the true Messiah: Jesus. Moreover, to have favor among all the people, one has to be known by all the people. That may seem too obvious, but in our day and age, it is something to be considered. People who did not yet know Jesus were acquainted with those who did. They had relationships with them. The church was not constantly isolated in some private gathering. No, the church engaged the culture around it intentionally, and God blessed the church's efforts.

Acts 5:42

Acts 2 is not the only place we see such engagement. Consider Acts 5:42: "And every day, in the temple and from house to house, they did not cease teaching and preaching that the Christ is Jesus."[2] Here, Luke removed any doubt that their engagement was not just to build friendships, but to reach people for Jesus and bring them into a personal relationship with him. In the same pattern as noted before, every day the early church was teaching and preaching the gospel about Jesus Christ in homes and in the temple. They were consistently engaging not only with religious seekers, but with friends and neighbors in the community. This engagement took intentionality. It took planning. It took time. It took consistency and commitment. Their approach was not coincidental.

Acts 16:13–15

Another example of their engagement is seen in Acts 16:

> And on the Sabbath day we [Paul and his traveling companions][3] went outside the gate to the riverside, where we supposed there was a place of prayer, and we sat down and spoke to the women who had come together. One who heard us was a woman named Lydia, from the city of Thyatira, a seller of purple goods, who was a worshiper of God. The Lord opened her heart to pay attention to what was said

---

[2]   See also Acts 5:19–21, where the apostles have been arrested and are in prison: "But during the night an angel of the Lord opened the prison doors and brought them out, and said, 'Go and stand in the temple and speak to the people all the words of this Life.' And when they heard this, they entered the temple at daybreak and began to teach."

[3]   Mark and Luke seem to be among them. Others may well have been in the group.

by Paul. And after she was baptized, and her household as well, she urged us, saying, "If you have judged me to be faithful to the Lord, come to my house and stay." And she prevailed upon us. (vv. 13–15)

Paul and his team went outside the city to the riverside on the Sabbath. Why? They presumed people would go there to pray. They strategically picked a place where spiritually curious people would likely be present so they might have a spiritual conversation with those who had yet to encounter the resurrected Jesus. Once again, not only at the beginning of the church, but throughout its development, we see a pattern of intentional engagement with the culture for the sake of winning others to Jesus. We see the early church engaging others where they are in the midst of daily life and religious habits. This passage also shows the fruit of these encounters: Lydia put her faith in Jesus!

Acts 19:8–10

One final example comes from Acts 19:

And [Paul] entered the synagogue and for three months spoke boldly, reasoning and persuading them about the kingdom of God. But when some became stubborn and continued in unbelief, speaking evil of the Way before the congregation, he withdrew from them and took the disciples with him, reasoning daily in the hall of Tyrannus. This continued for two years, so that all the residents of Asia heard the word of the Lord, both Jews and Greeks. (vv. 8–10)

Synagogues played an important social and religious role in the lives of the Jews scattered throughout the Roman Empire during this time. They were generally equipped with a platform for the reading of the Hebrew or Old Testament Scriptures, instructions and sermons based on the reading, congregational exhortations, and prayers.[4] After three months of Paul's participating in the activities of the synagogue and teaching attendees about the kingdom of God, some members became angry and hindered the advancement of the gospel there. What did Paul do? Did he quit? No. When the door closed at the synagogue, he moved on, shaking the dust off his feet (see Matt 10:14). He

---

4   Matthew E. Gordley, "Synagogue," in *The Lexham Bible Dictionary*, ed. John D. Barry et al. (Bellingham, WA: Lexham, 2016); C. L. Feinberg, "Synagogue," *New Bible Dictionary*, ed. D. R. W. Wood et al. (Downers Grove, IL: InterVarsity Press, 1996), 1142; and Paul J. Achtemeier, ed., with the Society of Biblical Literature, *Harper's Bible Dictionary* (San Francisco: Harper & Row, 1985), 1007.

soon found another viable cultural option for engaging people with the truths of Jesus: the hall of Tyrannus. Now, we do not know a lot about this hall. It has been speculated that it was a lecture hall or school open to people seeking shelter from the day's heat.[5] It would not have been uncommon for merchants and others to take an extended break during the hottest part of the day. Whatever the exact nature and function of the hall, it was a place familiar to the inhabitants of Ephesus where Paul could freely teach as a disciple of Jesus. These are the actions of a man driven to share an important message with others. Paul did not leave these encounters to chance. He and others in the early church did not just sit back and wait for an opportunity to come to them. Rather, Paul faithfully, consistently, and intentionally engaged the culture.

Spontaneous Engagement

The passages presented in the previous section demonstrated a planned approach to engagement by Christians. They were strategic. At the same time, other glimpses of the early church's engagements in Acts seemed to arise spontaneously, through everyday interactions. These encounters occurred because the early church was thoughtful and sensitive to the circumstances around them, as if their spiritual eyes and ears were alert for an opportunity to engage. They carefully listened to and looked at others around them as they functioned in this world, then engaged them. Here is one example:

> And it happened that while Apollos was at Corinth, Paul passed through the inland country and came to Ephesus. There he found some disciples. And he said to them, "Did you receive the Holy Spirit when you believed?" And they said, "No, we have not even heard that there is a Holy Spirit." And he said, "Into what then were you baptized?" They said, "Into John's baptism." And Paul said, "John baptized with the baptism of repentance, telling the people to believe in the one who was to come after him, that is, Jesus." On hearing this, they were baptized in the name of the Lord Jesus. And when Paul had laid his hands on them, the Holy Spirit came on them, and they began speaking in tongues and prophesying. There were about twelve men in all. (Acts 19:1–7)

---

5   Warren Johnson, "Tyrannus, Hall of," in Barry et al., *The Lexham Bible Dictionary*.

This passage comes immediately before Paul reasoned in the synagogue and then in the hall of Tyrannus. Remember that those were intentionally planned encounters, where Paul strategically engaged the culture with the gospel. However, the interaction Luke described here is different. It was spontaneous. Paul had just arrived in Ephesus when he came across some religious folks who believed in God generically, but did not know Jesus specifically. He did not appear to be looking for these people but came across them in the course of his missionary travels and struck up a conversation. These men were disciples of John the Baptist. Paul knew they were religious but did not know much about their faith, so he asked some questions. Based on their answers, Paul recognized that while they had a notion of God, they had missed his Son, Jesus. As Paul shared the good news with them, they quietly placed their faith in Jesus, were baptized, and received the Holy Spirit. This incredible encounter was not planned, but Paul was not going to miss out once it arose.

Consistently, Paul and others leveraged the cultural situation in order to effectively engage others for the purpose of sharing the gospel of Jesus Christ. As Paul himself wrote:

> For though I am free from all, I have made myself a servant to all, that I might win more of them. To the Jews I became as a Jew, in order to win Jews. To those under the law I became as one under the law (though not being myself under the law) that I might win those under the law. To those outside the law I became as one outside the law (not being outside the law of God but under the law of Christ) that I might win those outside the law. To the weak I became weak, that I might win the weak. I have become all things to all people, that by all means I might save some. I do it all for the sake of the gospel, that I may share with them in its blessings. (1 Cor 9:19–23)

The early church's model for engaging with the culture involved faithfully having conversations about Jesus in the normal course of life. They shared the truth about Jesus everywhere: from the temple, to their neighbors' houses, to the Jewish synagogues, and the marketplaces in pagan cities and villages.[6]

---

[6]   See also Acts 3:1–26; 5:20–21, 25; 8:25, 26–38, 40; 10:17–48; 13:5, 14–41; 14:1; 17:1–4, 10–12, 17; 18:4, 19, 26; 21:39–22:21, and elsewhere.

A Biblical Call

All these examples demonstrate that we are called to consistently engage our culture with the gospel in mind. We should do this both within and outside of our normal routines. For example, we might get outside of our routine and

- go on a mission trip,
- go door-to-door to people we do not know to engage them with a gospel conversation, or
- get another Christian family together and go to five houses a week in our neighborhood until we have hit every door, saying, "Hey, I know this might seem strange, but we just wanted to know if there is anything we can pray about with you."

We should certainly do these kinds of things, but that is only part of being an engaging church. We do not stop our cultural engagement there. We should desire, as the early church did, to engage all the time in all venues in all ways. We can engage in our everyday and every-weekend moments, and we can do it together. We can get together with other Christians with like interests and

- pray about how to engage the community together,
- fast together for the same end, and
- choose an engagement avenue on which to focus, being open to other ways to engage as well. (Look for places where curious people are already gathering and seek to meet them there.)

Whatever we do, our engagement should be natural and not forced.

Look to partner with other believers. If no one else is available, you commit to being an engaging person. Assess your already busy schedule. Are there activities in which you are already involved where you could just shift your mindset to be more intentional about sharing the gospel? It would take no more time from your schedule, just a commitment to see your responsibility and involvement differently. Another option might be to find common areas of interest. What do you like to do? Consider being involved with others who also enjoy those things, and engage. It should not be weird. Your engagement should be a natural outflow of like interests and genuine concern. As you engage with others, doors will open and conversations will take place. For example, consider engaging your world through . . .

- the school board, booster club, or parent-teacher association;
- a fantasy football league;
- getting to know the other parents involved with your kid's sports team;
- your homeowners' association;
- a shared workplace; or
- a classroom.

Effectively engaging with others through these avenues requires a missional mentality. God has called you to make disciples of others (Matt 28:19–20). Every venue, every relationship is an opportunity to live out the Christian life before others and to engage them kindly, looking for opportunities to talk to them about Jesus and their walk with God. You do not have to have all the answers; you just have to shift from distinguishing between everyday activities and missionary activities. Everyday activities can become missionary activities. Everyday conversations can be missionary conversations. That does not mean you push Jesus into every conversation; it means you have the gospel and your call to make disciples at the forefront of your mind as you engage others in these activities. It means you know your purpose in these activities is ultimately more than just filling a volunteer spot or finding a new friend. Pray about

- inviting people over for a cookout, where you can be a positive witness and look for opportunities in the conversation to talk about your faith;
- fishing, hunting, playing cards, or going to the movies with others, and seeking opportunities to talk about Jesus during your time together; or
- volunteering at a local charity or social service provider while seeking to be an encouragement to those around you and finding out where workers or recipients are in their faith.

Here are two pieces of practical advice as you go about engaging your culture. First, be careful about inviting people who are going to be a stumbling block to you. Second, engage your world alongside godly friends, so you can hold one another accountable to ensure that you are influencing the world, rather than the world influencing you.

A Deeper Engagement

You may already be engaging your world where you are. Maybe you are reaching out to friends on social media. Alternatively, you are talking to neighbors about life, yard work, and raising kids. Perhaps you are hanging out at your kids' ball games and talking to concession workers and other parents, or you have gotten to know the teller at your bank. We could possibly list a thousand other ways you are engaging your culture already because each believer functions within a different social context. But remember: we are talking about going deeper than a mere social engagement.

The engagement described in Acts is more than just getting to know others. We need to ensure that we have a gospel mindset. Instead of just being friendly, we are additionally looking for opportunities (open doors) to point people to Christ and gauge their level of openness to the gospel.

I (Adam) regularly have the opportunity to engage in everyday conversations with the gospel in mind at my kids' ball games. Once, in the course of a casual conversation on a Sunday afternoon, I asked a guy how his weekend was going. He talked about how busy his family had been and then mentioned that they had missed church that morning. I asked him where he went to church. (This would be a natural question to ask. It was not forced or weird. It did not come across as prying into his life. He did not feel as if I was trying to sell him something or recruit him into a multilevel marketing opportunity. It flowed with the conversation.) He chuckled and said, "Well, that's an interesting development. We are thinking about attending a Catholic church even though I was raised Baptist." That is a big shift. There are substantial differences there. Obviously, the man was spiritually searching and questioning some beliefs. I told him this was a big decision considering that the two groups can have wildly differing views of salvation. Throughout the conversation, I was able to work in the gospel in a nutshell and find out about his family and their thoughts regarding religion and faith. I thanked him for being so open. In certain parts of the world, I told him, people are killed for talking about different religious views, while in America we often do not even attempt to talk that personally with others. I appreciated his thoughtfulness, applauded his openness, and told him that I would be glad to talk further anytime. Later in the season, I was able to follow up on our previous conversation by simply asking for an update.

Around that same time, another parent shared with my wife that she was struggling in her marriage. My wife and I were able to encourage her and provide counsel. We have since built a friendly relationship with her. Throughout our conversations, we have shared the gospel and other biblical truths repeatedly in a kind and casual way.

As you engage others and build relationships, opportunities will inevitably open up whereby you can take the conversation deeper. Often, a crisis, a struggle, work troubles, financial stress, a car breaking down, a family death, a marriage issue, an injury, or some other issue will arise in a person's life. In these times, people talk. They seek advice. They search for spiritual truth. Over time, doors will open. Because you have shown you care and because you have common interests, people will tend to listen when you talk. Our goal should be to engage social issues, personal issues, and church issues, all with a gospel focus. We engage people out of a love for them, a love of God, and a heart that desires that all people experience redemption in Jesus.

Like our kids' sporting events, is there someplace in your life where you regularly interact with others? Can you engage them there with the gospel? For example, you could engage people on the soccer field with gospel intention. Have conversations with them. Build relationships. Love others, and help when needed. By the time a relationship has been built, they will have recognized that you are a believer in Jesus. (If they have not noticed, you may need to examine your life to see how evidentially you are living for Christ.) If they have not brought up the difference Jesus makes in your life, there are many ways you can naturally incorporate your faith and questions about their faith into the conversation. At lulls in the conversation, ask specific questions. When an opportunity arises, share your testimony. Just be sure to balance between asking good questions out of a genuine interest in them and sharing about your own life. As you get to know others, you can also invite them to join you at your church gathering. Do not assume that people are believers if they already go to church somewhere. Also, be sure that you do not end your spiritual investment with an invitation to a church gathering. We are not called to invite people to a church gathering or even get people to come to our church gathering; rather, we are called to make disciples by leading people to faith in Jesus and helping them mature in their walk with him. For the remainder of this chapter, we want to provide some specific advice to help you biblically engage.

Three *Be*'s of Engagement

1. Be Prepared

As previously demonstrated, some engagement opportunities in the early church were intentionally planned, and others arose spontaneously within the ebb and flow of life. Opportunities will arise for us to go on a planned local outreach, to a downtown mission, or on a mission trip. We may also simply plan to invite people over for dinner. These are all examples of planned engagement. There will also be times when we are standing in line at the grocery store or getting coffee with a coworker when an opportunity presents itself to engage someone about Jesus. These opportunities for engagement are more spontaneous. Both are important and should be part of our engagement mentality.

Regardless of whether the opportunity is planned or spontaneous, we must be prepared to notice doors when they open. We must be prepared for the encounter. We also must be walking in the Spirit and trusting in him to work through us. After all, the Holy Spirit is the one who opens the eyes of the lost and converts the sinner. He is also the one who comforts and convicts the saint.

Preparation for engagement is essential. Too many opportunities are missed because, when they arose, we did not feel adequate for the moment. We, all too often, allow our lack of preparedness to keep us from walking through the open door. So, as you seek to follow the example of the early church and prepare to engage the lost, consider these things:

Material. In the fall of 2015, an older friend of mine and a seasoned fisherman invited me fishing. It was a cool, rainy day. We did not catch many fish, but we had a great time being outside and encouraging one another. When the day was near an end, we headed back to the dock and loaded up the boat. As we prepared to leave, a game warden from the conservation department stopped us. They were tracking the number and type of fish caught in the lake so they could better manage the lake for generations to come. Due to the situation (there was a line of trucks behind us, waiting for us to get out of the way), my friend could not take a lot of time, but during the course of the warden's questions, my friend simply engaged in pleasant conversation, made a comment appropriate to the moment about his faith, and then invited the warden to church. He then reached in his truck and pulled out a card with the church's name, address, phone number, and website. This is an example of being prepared with material. It is not complicated or cumbersome.

Christians who attend public school have regular opportunities to have spiritual conversations with others. My own children have shared many stories concerning the varied beliefs of other students with whom they go to school. Some of these students call themselves "Christians," but they do not understand the basics of the gospel message. In school, you can carry a brochure on how to have a relationship with God to give out if the conversation runs short,[7] or you can meet and do research to help answer their questions. In short, there are many resources that can help you engage the culture. Be prepared with material.

Memorization. To be fully prepared to engage people for Christ, we need to have some information committed to memory. We will not always have access to printed or electronic material. Time and circumstances do not always allow for that. Therefore, we must have certain Bible verses memorized that will enable us to walk someone through a gospel presentation should the opportunity arise. Along with these verses, it is often helpful to have a gospel paradigm to walk people through. Such systems, committed to memory, can enable you to share the gospel in seconds or hours, depending on the moment and what time allows. There are two easy systems you can use. Pray through and find the one with which you are most comfortable, and then, commit that one to memory. You will find a lot of overlap in these two.

The first system is known as the Romans Road because all the verses are taken from the book of Romans.

- Everyone is a sinner and guilty before God. Romans 3:23 reveals that "all have sinned and fall short of the glory of God."
- The penalty for our sin is spiritual death. Romans 6:23: "For the wages of sin is death, but the free gift of God is eternal life in Christ Jesus our Lord."
- While we were in sin and deserving of death, God sent his Son, Jesus, to die for us. Romans 5:8: "God shows his love for us in that while we were still sinners, Christ died for us."
- God made a way for our sin to be paid for. For all who believe, Jesus has offered to take our penalty upon himself. Romans 8:1: "Therefore, there is now no condemnation for those in Christ Jesus."
- We only have to believe that Jesus died and rose again as our substitute, paying for our sins to be saved from the wages of sin.

---

7   The North American Mission Board (NAMB) has an incredible app called the 3 Circles: Life Conversation Guide that you can use to have gospel conversations with people. They also have printed material. See Life on Mission, http://lifeonmissionbook.com/conversation-guide. Additionally, Living Waters ministry has some resources you may find helpful: https://www.livingwaters.com/.

Romans 10:9–10: "If you confess with your mouth that Jesus is Lord and believe in your heart that God raised him from the dead, you will be saved. For with the heart one believes and is justified, and with the mouth one confesses and is saved."

Memorizing six verses (Rom 3:23; 5:8; 6:23; 8:1; and 10:9–10) will enable you to walk someone through these steps.

Here is another system, which I (Adam) refer to as the four Ps. This system is presented in much greater detail with many more verses in chapter 1 of *Square One: Back to the Basics*:[8]

- God's **P**erfection. God is holy and perfect. Leviticus 19:2: "You shall be holy, for I the LORD your God am holy."
- God's **P**roblem. Because God is holy, he will not tolerate sin. This poses a problem for us because "all have sinned and fall short of the glory of God" (Rom 3:23).
- God's **P**rovision. God, in his love, grace, and mercy, made a provision for our sin. Romans 5:8: "God shows his love for us in that while we were still sinners, Christ died for us."
- God's **P**romise. God promises that all who accept Jesus as their substitute sacrifice and believe in his name will be forgiven of their sin and restored to a right relationship with God. John 1:12: "But to all who did receive [Jesus], who believed in his name, he gave the right to become children of God."

We can also be prepared by knowing how the Bible answers common questions people have regarding the Christian faith.[9] When you have a conversation and someone raises a question you are unprepared to answer, go home and study. Memorize these types of questions and biblical answers to them.

Another way we can be prepared is by memorizing people's names. If you meet new people at the gym or a work gathering, try to memorize their names, or at least save them in a specific place, such

---

[8]   Adam McClendon and Matt Kimbrough, *Square One: Back to the Basics* (Little Elm, TX: eLectio, 2018), 3–17.

[9]   Some of what we are describing as "engaging others" may sound like apologetics to some of our readers. There is certainly overlap, and if you are interested in a more specific model/method for apologetics as cultural engagement, we recommend Joshua Chatraw and Mark Allen, *Apologetics at the Cross* (Grand Rapids: Zondervan, 2018). This text also very helpfully deals with a number of "defeaters" of the Christian faith.

as the notes app on your phone, with a brief description that you can review before seeing them again. Then, when you are about to be in a social context where they might be present, review your list of names and descriptions. Calling someone by name when you are having a conversation and building a relationship communicates that you are interested in and care about that person. This simple act shows that you value the people you are engaging.

Mindset. We also need to be prepared in mindset. Just living life and waiting for things to happen is simply not good enough. We need to be prepared. Before we ever walk into an opportunity to engage others, we should think about how we would respond in different situations, how we would answer certain questions, and what we might say if the opportunity to share the gospel arises. This is engagement with a gospel purpose. If you are with a fellow parent at a Sunday sports practice, ask that parent if he or she had to miss church. Then you can ask, "Where do you go to church?" If nowhere, ask if he or she is interested in your church and what you believe. If someone is struggling in marriage, ask her if she is praying and if you can pray for her. Ask her if she believes God has a plan for her, and be prepared to share God's plan. If someone tells you he quit church because of hypocrites, say something like, "You have obviously been hurt," and ask him what happened. These approaches are not an end in themselves. They are bridges that help you connect with others, learn more about them, and hopefully, be able to eventually reach them with the gospel if they are lost or encourage them in their faith if they are believers. The key is to be prepared to have honest conversations with people and to be ready to make a defense to anyone who asks you for a reason for the hope that is in you (1 Pet 3:15).

2. Be Patient

Next, it is important to be patient. Relationships take time, lots of time. We cannot rush true relationship. Here are a couple of things to remember as we strive to be patient in the face of complicated relationships.

Focus on caring before curing. Our ultimate goal is to share the gospel of Jesus with those we engage; however, we often must focus first on caring for and loving those around us before we seek to cure their ultimate disease—sin—with the gospel of Jesus Christ. Henri Nouwen says:

Our tendency is to run away from the painful realities or to try and change them as soon as possible. But cure without care makes us into rulers, controllers, manipulators, and prevents a real community from taking shape. Cure without care makes us preoccupied with quick changes, impatient and unwilling to share each other's burden. And so cure can often become offending instead of liberating. It is therefore not so strange that cure is not seldom refused by people in need. Not only have individuals refused help when they did not sense a real care, but also oppressed nations have declined medicine and food when they realized that it was better to suffer than to lose self-respect by accepting a gift out of a non-caring hand.[10]

Our care for those we are engaging will generally need to come first, but all the while with a gospel mindset, looking for opportunities to share the life we have found in Jesus.

At a spiritual retreat, I came across a young man who had struggled with suicidal thoughts and was trying to deal with some addiction issues. As he shared with me over dinner, all I really wanted to do was get back to my retreat; but the very thing with which he was struggling, I had been studying. The Lord convicted me, and I ended up just spending time listening and genuinely sympathizing. In the course of the conversation, I was able to share the gospel. The man claimed to be a Christian and to believe in the gospel already, so I encouraged him to live more passionately and faithfully for Christ. My words had power in his life in the end because of the genuine and patient interest I had taken in him. My caring opened a door for some curing to take place.

God will cure; you care and look for open doors. It is ultimately not our responsibility to cure others. We are simply called to care and present the cure, Jesus. We are to be there when people are in need and point them to the cross. We are called to consistently love sacrificially and model Jesus to them (1 Cor 11:1). We need to be paying close

---

10   Henri Nouwen, *Out of Solitude* (Notre Dame, IN: Ave Maria, 2004), 37.

attention to see the open doors to serve well. God will provide opportunities for us to love and serve others for the purpose of us sharing our heavenly hope with them. We need to take those opportunities. We often get frustrated because we want instantaneous results whether or not the person is ready for the truth and change we are presenting.

On Monday, June 11, 2012, I made this note in my journal.

I'm unbelievably humbled by the private social media message I received this morning. Over the last few months, God has been continually stirring within me a renewed passion for the gospel. May it never cease! Here is the message I received:

Adam, you probably won't remember me but I used to work at the Riverchase Galleria when you worked at Verizon . . . My hair was a lot shorter. I will never forget the day you walked with me to the food court and asked me straight up if I died how did I know if I was going to heaven? I remember my answer that I would go to heaven because I was a good person. Then you explained to me that it was about Christ's death on the cross and repenting and calling on Him and embracing Him by faith. I think it was in '99 when I started reading my Bible every day and I have not put it down since. I owe you my life like Paul was sarcastically saying to Philemon about Onesimus. I am amazed that I could remember your whole name and your wife's name. Seriously though I had been in church for 18 yrs of my life and never knew about Jesus or having an intimate relationship with Him. . . . I have been at . . . Church now for almost 13 yrs. The Lord is my life and the length of my days—not just a number on a list of priorities. I'd be lost without Him. There is no way I'd have made it this far. I have been through SO much trial along the way but I can still say no matter what that I will extol the Lord at all times and His praise will continually be on my lips. I have gone through the loss of my firstborn daughter and have had a difficult marriage to say the least. . . . Anyway, I just never got to thank you for telling me the gospel. I haven't shut up yet about Him! . . . But thank you!!!!

Just reading this post again stirs my heart and reminds me of God's faithfulness to bring about good fruit when the seed of the gospel falls on fertile soil (see Matt 13:1–9, 18–23). God wants faithful laborers who will sow seed and wait patiently for the fruits of our labor. This is how we are patient in our engagement.

3. Be Yourself

When you are intentionally engaging others, it is so important to be prepared and to be patient, but you should also just be yourself. Do not try to be your pastor, a professor, or anyone else you are not. Do not be fake. Be yourself. You can do this. You were created for this. God has called you to this. You are wonderful just as God made you. You are adequately equipped for the opportunities God has placed before you. Trust that God wants to use you to do the work you were created to do, and then, get out there and do it. Remember that you are not a Bible salesperson. It is not your job to "sweeten the deal." The Holy Spirit does the work of convicting. Your role is simply to engage with a gospel mindset and take advantage of opportunities to speak about Jesus.

Final Thoughts

We do not need more church programming. We need more believers engaging our world. If we can live out this vision of ministry presented throughout Acts, it will revolutionize our pastimes, our online activities, our recreation, our social interactions, and the way we view our world. We exist to engage our culture, in every arena, with a gospel mindset; and if we buy into this vision, each of us will find a natural and biblical way to make an impact through gospel engagement.

Personal Reflection or Group Discussion Questions

1. Before reading this chapter, what was your conception of engaging with others? How has that conception changed or been reaffirmed?

2. What does it mean to engage with others? Why is engagement important, and what is our biblical mandate for doing so?

3. How do you currently engage with the world within your daily, monthly, and yearly routines? What are some specific ways you can intentionally engage the world with the gospel in mind?

4. How do you currently engage with the world outside of your routines? What are some specific ways you can intentionally engage the world outside of your routines?

5. Review the first *Be* of engagement: "Be Prepared." How prepared are you for planned or spontaneous gospel engagements? On which of the preparations listed do you need to work?

6. In what ways do you or can you practice patience in your engagement? What is the danger of impatience? Have you ever seen impatience ruin a relationship? How?

Devotional

Day One: Acts 2:46–47

How do you consistently engage others? Do you have favor in your community?

Open your Bible and read Acts 2:46–47.

In this passage, we see the early Christians engaging with one another and with their community on a consistent basis.

Think deeply about the following questions:

Do you participate in practices with other believers and with your community in ways similar to the early Christians? How can you better integrate this kind of engagement into your particular context? What would this look like in your life?

In your engagement with the community, do you have favor with all people? Should this be sought? What does it actually mean that the early church had "favor with all the people"? What should this look like today?

This passage models engaging within routine. Engaging within routine happens in two ways: (1) in the community, and (2) in the home. How can you engage in the community? How can you welcome others into your home and engage with them there?

This kind of ministry can be costly. What are the risks of inviting others into your home? Why is gospel-minded ministry worth the risk?

What seems to be the result of this gospel-minded engagement according to the passage? Is that result guaranteed for us? What should be our expectation for success?

Devotional

Day Two: Acts 8:25–39

Have you ever shared the gospel with someone? What role did the Bible play in the discussion?

Open your Bible and read Acts 8:25–39.

In this passage, Philip engages with an Ethiopian eunuch and takes advantage of the opportunity laid before him by the Holy Spirit to share the gospel.

Think deeply about the following questions:

Where did this interaction take place? What was Philip doing before it? Why was he able to take advantage of this opportunity?

How did Philip know to be in the right place at the right time? While we probably should not expect to hear the audible voice of the Lord in our everyday experiences, we do need to be walking in the Spirit. How does one "walk in the Spirit"? What does that look like in daily life?

There were class and economic differences between Philip and the Ethiopian. How willing are you to break those barriers to engage others? How often do you speak to people outside your own socioeconomic sector?

How did Philip engage the eunuch? What role did Scripture play? How can Scripture play a greater role in your engagement?

Devotional

Day Three: Acts 10

How obedient would you say you are to the government? Society? Your friends? Your spouse's expectations? Your boyfriend or girlfriend's expectations?

Open your Bible and read Acts 10.

Acts 10 presents a powerful example of an early Christian following God somewhere he did not want to go for the sake of the gospel.

Think deeply about the following questions:

Why was Peter told to go see Cornelius? What was the separation between them? In other words, why did Peter not want to go see him?

How might God be calling you to cross boundaries for the sake of his gospel?

What was the result of Peter's willingness to go in the end? What might God have for others on the other side of your obedience?

Devotional

Day Four: Acts 16:11–15

Are you aware of a time when the Holy Spirit used your witness to bring someone to repentance? If so, what was the situation? If not, what do you think that would be like?

Open your Bible and read Acts 16:11–15.

In this passage, we see a businesswoman named Lydia come to know Christ under Paul's preaching.

Think deeply about the following questions:

With the gospel in mind, with whom is God moving you to engage? How might you share the gospel with these people?

In this passage, as in the story of Philip and the Ethiopian, there are cultural boundaries between the early Christians and those with whom they engage. Lydia is well-to-do, and many in the early church were not, yet God used them to lead Lydia to repentance. Have you ever been burdened for someone, but then immediately rejected the possibility of his or her salvation for one reason or another? We have to realize the power of the gospel and the supernatural working of God in salvation. How can you share the gospel with those you have previously thought of as "beyond reach"? Are any of them above you in socioeconomic status? Are they in a lower class financially or educationally? Do not let that stop you from engaging with them and looking for opportunities for gospel conversations.

Where did Paul and those traveling with him speak to the women in Acts 16:11–15? Can you think of a similar, parallel context in your community? How could you engage these folks in your own community?

Lydia, the new believer, invited Paul and the others into her home. How can you leverage your home this week for the sake of the gospel? What kind of engagement can you do there?

Devotional

Day Five: Acts 19:1–10

Have you ever tried to engage with others, even to the point of sharing the gospel, and gotten pushback? What was the situation?

Open your Bible and read Acts 19:1–10.

In this passage, we see Paul preaching with mixed results, but even in the midst of rejection, he continued to engage others faithfully.

Think deeply about the following questions:

How did Paul know these disciples were not followers of Jesus? What does this insight suggest about our engagement opportunities?

Where did Paul go next to engage others? Where is a similar public place today? How can you engage there?

What was Paul's response when he encountered stubbornness, unbelief, and gossip? Did he stop engaging? Did he leave the city? Did he simply go elsewhere in the area with the gospel? How might Paul's practice look in our own lives?

How should we respond when we are faced with pushback against the gospel?

CONCLUSION

Have you ever read a description of the events of a ball game after the fact? Have you ever tried to envision what the game must have been like, how the tension and excitement built in the stadium, what smells would be present, and how the players and fans reacted? This is almost impossible if you weren't actually there! In the same way, it is next to impossible to truly understand the church without being there. Throughout the book, we have examined five characteristics of the early church from the book of Acts and attempted to explain them and show their importance for today. Nevertheless, if you have not truly experienced the local church firsthand, it is hard to understand fully the value of the institution and its people. So where do we go from here? Get involved in a local church. Find a spiritual family who will love, exhort, confess, and forgive with you. Try to get involved with a confessing, gathering, giving, engaging, and praying church and strive to faithfully live these characteristics out in the community as well. If a local church is slightly deficient in one of these areas, maybe you can be the change agent that pushes the church to be more faithful. Get involved and become a member!

You have reached the end of this book, but thank God, it is not the end for the church. We hope your heart has been reignited for God's church. Our prayer from the beginning has been that God would use this work to build and edify his church. We also pray that your love for the church does not grow cold as you close this book but that it will continue to grow and burn brightly as you commune with the body of Christ.

APPENDIX

P.R.A.Y. MODEL FOR PRAYER

Sometimes it is helpful to have a systemized way to walk through
a prayer. This approach is often beneficial whether praying alone
or praying with others. It helps focus our mind on categories.
One systemized way to pray is by using the acronym P.R.A.Y.

P stands for **Praise.**

In this portion of the prayer, you acknowledge the greatness of God and offer praise for who he is, what he has done, and what he is going to do.

R stands for **Repent.**

In this portion of the prayer, you acknowledge your sin and need for Jesus. You ask for the strength and humility to turn from your sin and live more faithfully by the power of the Spirit for Jesus.

A stands for **Ask.**

In this portion of the prayer, you simply make various requests based on the needs and desires you have.

Y stands for **Yield.**

In this portion of the prayer, you simply yield your life and requests to God. You acknowledge that there are times you ask in ignorance for things that may not be best for your life and the glory of God. You acknowledge that you may at times ask for things with the wrong motives. In the end, you submit yourself to the Lord and ask him to answer these prayers according to his will in accomplishing his purposes.

PRIVATE OR
CORPORATE PRAYER GUIDES

Prayer Meeting Template (P.R.A.Y.)

P - Praise

Let us work to delight in God.

1 Peter 1:3–5: "Blessed be the God and Father of our Lord Jesus Christ! According to his great mercy, he has caused us to be born again to a living hope through the resurrection of Jesus Christ from the dead, to an inheritance that is imperishable, undefiled, and unfading, kept in heaven for you, who by God's power are being guarded through faith for a salvation ready to be revealed in the last time."

We have lots to praise him for. God is . . .

- eternal
- triune
- perfect
- all-powerful
- all-knowing
- all-present
- self-existent
- sovereign
- wise
- Creator
- loving
- gracious
- merciful
- kind
- good
- just
- holy
- righteous
- forgiving
- patient

We have . . .

- redemption provided in Jesus Christ;
- a future inheritance that is imperishable, undefiled, unfading, and secure; and
- the privilege to serve as a gospel witness.

R - Repent
Let us seek to be the holy people he has called us to be.

1 Peter 1:13–16: "Therefore, preparing your minds for action, and being sober-minded, set your hope fully on the grace that will be brought to you at the revelation of Jesus Christ. As obedient children, do not be conformed to the passions of your former ignorance, but as he who called you is holy, you also be holy in all your conduct, since it is written, 'You shall be holy, for I am holy.'"

We are called to be holy, so . . .

- confess personal sins, even publicly.
- confess corporate sins (the sins prevalent in the body).
- confess societal sins (the sins prevalent in the world around us).
- acknowledge the holiness of God.
- acknowledge that we need God's purifying presence and power.

Some common sins are these:

- sins of speech (slander, gossip, profanity, vulgarity)
- lust
- anger
- greed
- envy
- impatience

A - Ask
Let us approach holy God in prayer while keeping his coming kingdom in view.

1 Peter 4:7: "The end of all things is at hand; therefore be self-controlled and sober-minded for the sake of your prayers."

What do you want to ask God for? He is a good, faithful, and sovereign Father.

Some specific requests for us as a church:

- for fruitful mission trips
- to help our sick to keep their eyes on Christ and serve as a gospel witness while fighting illness
- for preservation of our religious freedom, which is quickly eroding
- for holiness, and for the power to live repentant lives
- for guests to feel connected and welcome
- for God to continue to provide finances
- for volunteers to have strength, energy, balance, wisdom, and joy in their service to the Lord
- that lives continue to be transformed for the gospel, and for more salvations this year
- for new members to get connected quickly and experience community
- that the Word of God would be preached rightly and fall on hearts ready to change and be sustained by God's Spirit
- for success in our upcoming events
- for staff and their families

Y - Yield

Let us entrust our souls to our sovereign God, seeking for his will to be done and his kingdom to come.

1 Peter 4:19: "Therefore let those who suffer according to God's will entrust their souls to a faithful Creator while doing good."

Together, let's acknowledge our ultimate submission to Christ and our ultimate trust in his decisions. Let us also demonstrate that we surrender to his will—he can answer these requests in his fashion, and we will still worship him.

Prayer Meeting Template (A.C.T.S.)

A - Adoration

Psalm 113:1–3: "Praise the LORD! Praise, O servants of the LORD, praise the name of the LORD! Blessed be the name of the LORD from this time forth and forevermore! From the rising of the sun to its setting, the name of the LORD is to be praised!"

C - Confession

Psalm 51:1–7: "Have mercy on me, O God, according to your steadfast love; according to your abundant mercy blot out my transgressions. Wash me thoroughly from my iniquity, and cleanse me from my sin! For I know my transgressions, and my sin is ever before me. Against you, you only, have I sinned and done what is evil in your sight, so that you may be justified in your words and blameless in your judgment. Behold, I was brought forth in iniquity, and in sin did my mother conceive me. Behold, you delight in truth in the inward being, and you teach me wisdom in the secret heart. Purge me with hyssop, and I shall be clean; wash me, and I shall be whiter than snow."

T - Thanksgiving

Psalm 107:1–3: "Oh give thanks to the LORD, for he is good, for his steadfast love endures forever! Let the redeemed of the LORD say so, whom he has redeemed from trouble and gathered in from the lands, from the east and from the west, from the north and from the south."

S - Supplication

Psalm 40:1–5: "I waited patiently for the LORD; he inclined to me and heard my cry. He drew me up from the pit of destruction, out of the miry bog, and set my feet upon a rock, making my steps secure. He put a new song in my mouth, a song of praise to our God. Many will see and fear, and put their trust in the LORD. Blessed is the man who makes the LORD his trust, who does not turn to the proud, to those who go astray after a lie! You have multiplied, O LORD my God, your wondrous deeds and your thoughts toward us; none can compare with you! I will proclaim and tell of them, yet they are more than can be told."

Prayer Meeting Template 1

Use these passages and titles to direct prayers.

Acknowledging who God is and what he has done . . .

Psalm 18:1–2, 31–35: "I love you, O LORD, my strength. The LORD is my rock and my fortress and my deliverer, my God, my rock, in whom I take refuge, my shield, and the horn of my salvation, my stronghold. . . . For who is God, but the LORD? And who is a rock, except our God?—the God who equipped me with strength and made my way blameless. He made my feet like the feet of a deer and set me secure on the heights. He trains my hands for war, so that my arms can bend a bow of bronze. You have given me the shield of your salvation, and your right hand supported me, and your gentleness made me great."

Confessing our unworthiness and need for grace . . .

Psalm 51:1–2, 7–10: "Have mercy on me, O God, according to your steadfast love; according to your abundant mercy blot out my transgressions. Wash me thoroughly from my iniquity, and cleanse me from my sin! . . . Purge me with hyssop, and I shall be clean; wash me, and I shall be whiter than snow. Let me hear joy and gladness; let the bones that you have broken rejoice. Hide your face from my sins, and blot out all my iniquities. Create in me a clean heart, O God, and renew a right spirit within me."

Interceding on behalf of the nations . . .

Psalm 22:27–28: "All the ends of the earth shall remember and turn to the LORD, and all the families of the nations shall worship before you. For kingship belongs to the LORD, and he rules over the nations."

Psalm 67:1–2: "May God be gracious to us and bless us and make his face to shine upon us, that your way may be known on earth, your saving power among all nations."

Interceding on behalf of the needy . . .

Psalm 9:18: "For the needy shall not always be forgotten, and the hope of the poor shall not perish forever."

Seeking God's protection and favor . . .

Psalm 5:7–12: "But I, through the abundance of your steadfast love, will enter your house. I will bow down toward your holy temple in the fear of you. Lead me, O Lord, in your righteousness because of my enemies; make your way straight before me. For there is no truth in their mouth; their inmost self is destruction; their throat is an open grave; they flatter with their tongue. Make them bear their guilt, O God; let them fall by their own counsels; because of the abundance of their transgressions cast them out, for they have rebelled against you. But let all who take refuge in you rejoice; let them ever sing for joy, and spread your protection over them, that those who love your name may exult in you. For you bless the righteous, O Lord; you cover him with favor as with a shield."

Thanking and praising God . . .

Psalm 92:1–4: "It is good to give thanks to the Lord, to sing praises to your name, O Most High; to declare your steadfast love in the morning, and your faithfulness by night, to the music of the lute and the harp, to the melody of the lyre. For you, O Lord, have made me glad by your work; at the works of your hands I sing for joy."

Prayer Meeting Template 2

Use these passages and titles to direct prayers.

1 Timothy 2:1–4: "First of all, then, I urge that supplications, prayers, inter-cessions, and thanksgivings be made for all people, for kings and all who are in high positions, that we may lead a peaceful and quiet life, godly and dignified in every way. This is good, and it is pleasing in the sight of God our Savior, who desires all people to be saved and to come to the knowledge of the truth."

- Pray for the country, government, officials, foreign governments

Matthew 9:36–38: "When he saw the crowds, he had compassion for them, because they were harassed and helpless, like sheep without a shepherd. Then he said to his disciples, 'The harvest is plentiful, but the laborers are few; therefore pray earnestly to the Lord of the harvest to send out laborers into his harvest.'"

- Pray for the lost, hurting, straying, faithful, and grounded

Matthew 5:43–47: "You have heard that it was said, 'You shall love your neigh-bor and hate your enemy.' But I say to you, Love your enemies and pray for those who persecute you, so that you may be sons of your Father who is in heaven. For he makes his sun rise on the evil and on the good, and sends rain on the just and on the unjust. For if you love those who love you, what reward do you have? Do not even the tax collectors do the same? And if you greet only your brothers, what more are you doing than others? Do not even the Gentiles do the same?"

- Pray for terrorists, jihadists, persecutors of the church, gospel-opposers, those whose positions you hate

James 5:16: "Therefore, confess your sins to one another and pray for one another, that you may be healed. The prayer of a righteous person has great power as it is working."

- Pray for anyone on your prayer list and others, the physically and spiritually broken

Prayer Meeting Template 3

Use these passages and titles to direct prayers.

The almighty God of the universe came to earth in human form to pay the penalty for our sin. He has brought good news to the afflicted, healed the brokenhearted, and set the captive free.

Perspective, Praise, and Repentance:
Romans 8:1: "There is therefore now no condemnation for those who are in Christ Jesus."

1 John 1:9: "If we confess our sins, he is faithful and just to forgive us our sins and to cleanse us from all unrighteousness."

Galatians 5:16: "But I say, walk by the Spirit, and you will not gratify the desires of the flesh."

Psalm 95:3: "For the LORD is a great God, and a great King above all gods."

Pray for . . .
- love for God alone to consume his people;
- a wave of repentance to demolish strongholds, tear down idols, and revive his church;
- the power of the Holy Spirit to flood the church and fill his people once again;
- total surrender to the call to advance his kingdom around the world; and
- a willingness and ability to authentically confess and repent of any wrongdoing, false dependencies, misplaced ideas, and loss of spiritual passion.

The Lost, Broken, Hurting, Hungry, and Homeless:
Psalm 96:3: "Declare his glory among the nations, his marvelous works among all the peoples!"

Luke 19:10: "For the Son of Man came to seek and to save the lost."

Pray for . . .
- lost friends and family;
- the lost who attend our churches, live in our neighborhoods, work with us, play on our sports teams, and attend our schools;
- missionaries and organizations striving to advance the gospel; and
- missionaries you currently partner with in [name the countries].

Proverbs 13:23: "The fallow ground of the poor would yield much food, but it is swept away through injustice."

Proverbs 14:20–21: "The poor is disliked even by his neighbor, but the rich has many friends. Whoever despises his neighbor is a sinner, but blessed is he who is generous to the poor."

Psalm 23:4: "Even though I walk through the valley of the shadow of death, I will fear no evil, for you are with me; your rod and your staff, they comfort me."

Pray for God to . . .
- show us how to respond to the growing needs of those around us in a way representative of the generosity we have been shown in the gospel
- give wisdom and resources to those agencies seeking to minister to the broken, hurting, and homeless in our communities

Leadership: (*Sunday School and Life Group Leaders, Deacons, Pastors, and Staff*) Ephesians 4:15: "Rather, speaking the truth in love, we are to grow up in every way into him who is the head, into Christ."

Pray that they will . . .
- be committed to their families with authentic love and care, that they will be strong and learn in the midst of trials, and that their homes will be a refuge and haven of rest
- become more surrendered and poured out to Christ, so they can have spiritual breakthroughs by seeking the fear of God and the mind of Christ and the Spirit's leading
- exhibit godly Christian character and integrity with all of their relationships and dealings in life
- will have the strength and endurance they need to serve with excellence by the power of the Spirit

2 Timothy 3:16–17: "All Scripture is breathed out by God and profitable for teaching, for reproof, for correction, and for training in righteousness, that the man of God may be complete, equipped for every good work."

2 Timothy 4:1–2: "I charge you in the presence of God and of Christ Jesus, who is to judge the living and the dead, and by his appearing and his kingdom: preach the word."

Pray that . . .
- the Word of God will never be compromised, cheapened, or dumbed down; rather, that it will be delivered in confidence with power, conviction, clarity, boldness, and love, and in truth
- worship is never a show, entertainment or talent focused, but rather that God is the audience of our praise

Church and Personal Life:
2 Corinthians 1:3–4: "Blessed be the God and Father of our Lord Jesus Christ, the Father of mercies and God of all comfort, who comforts us in all our affliction, so that we may be able to comfort those who are in any affliction, with the comfort with which we ourselves are comforted by God."

Pray that the church will . . .
- comfort those who have lost loved ones or are going through hard times in a way that draws them close to Christ and enables them to minister to others in the church
- be a community of grace and forgiveness, and that your church has an atmosphere of encouragement by being grateful for Christ's work, which enables us to be inspired to give genuine hospitality to all who come through our doors

Ephesians 4:32–5:1: "Be kind to one another, tenderhearted, forgiving one another, as God in Christ forgave you. Therefore be imitators of God, as beloved children."

Romans 15:5–6: "May the God of endurance and encouragement grant you to live in such harmony with one another, in accord with Christ Jesus, that together you may with one voice glorify the God and Father of our Lord Jesus Christ."

1 Peter 1:3–4: "Blessed be the God and Father of our Lord Jesus Christ! According to his great mercy, he has caused us to be born again to a living hope through the resurrection of Jesus Christ from the dead, to an inheritance that is imperishable, undefiled, and unfading, kept in heaven for you."

Pray . . .
- that each attendee will take hold of a growing, consistent walk with Christ through a steadfast devotional and prayer life;
- that each believer will realize that our inheritance and hope as a church family is in God's incomparable and incredible great power, which is available to us;
- that we will stand against gossip, negative criticism, false expectations, unhealthy burdens, strife, and weariness that will seek to invade the church family;
- for healing, forgiveness, and reconciliation for any misplaced expectations, criticism, ungrateful attitudes, flawed thinking, grief, hurts, and abuse;
- that unity infuses the church so that each congregation binds to Christ in love so the work of the kingdom is promoted;
- that genuine community is fostered through the various ministries of your church;
- that believers will remain faithful and good stewards, so financial needs are met; and
- that the body will grow a healthy understanding, wisdom, and handling of our finances and facilities, to better receive and manage God's blessings.

Galatians 6:14: "But far be it from me to boast except in the cross of our Lord Jesus Christ, by which the world has been crucified to me, and I to the world."

Pray that . . .
- our focus would be on the supremacy of Christ and that we will be dependent upon him
- we would be real, authentic disciples of Christ, who are learning, growing, and producing fruit, and in turn making more disciples

Matthew 25:36: "I was naked and you clothed me, I was sick and you visited me, I was in prison and you came to me."

James 5:13–14: "Is anyone among you suffering? Let him pray. Is anyone cheerful? Let him sing praise. Is anyone among you sick? Let him call for the elders of the church, and let them pray over him, anointing him with oil in the name of the Lord."

Pray for . . .
- the sick and the physical needs of the body

Acts 1:14: "All these with one accord were devoting themselves to prayer."

Acts 2:42: "And they devoted themselves to the apostles' teaching and the fellowship, to the breaking of bread and the prayers."

Pray that . . .
- all will draw near to Christ and seek holiness and his presence with more prayer
- we would receive God's direction and vision, and that we are nourished from the substance of his Word

Church Worldwide:
Psalm 10:2: "In arrogance the wicked hotly pursue the poor; let them be caught in the schemes that they have devised."

1 Peter 5:8: "Be sober-minded; be watchful. Your adversary the devil prowls around like a roaring lion, seeking someone to devour."

Matthew 8:11: "I tell you, many will come from east and west and recline at table with Abraham, Isaac, and Jacob in the kingdom of heaven."

Pray that . . .
- God will strengthen, sustain, and encourage those persecuted around the world for standing firm for the gospel of Jesus Christ;
- God will use their witness to turn the enemy's tactics against him so that those who attack God's people are convicted by the witness of the saints and as a result the persecutors end up repenting and converting to Christ; and that
- the church universal will expand and continue to grow in such a way that it is evident that the gates of hell cannot stand against her.

Prayer Meeting Template 4

Use these passages and titles to direct prayers.

"In prayer, we are not just spewing sporadic unfiltered emotional thoughts to a friend; we are also approaching a loving and holy God. It is important for us to temper our hearts for prayer so that our condition is shaped more by the presence of the one before whom we cry out than the circumstances in which we live." —Adam McClendon

1 Chronicles 4:8–10: "Koz fathered Anub, Zobebah, and the clans of Aharhel, the son of Harum. Jabez was more honorable than his brothers; and his mother called his name Jabez, saying, 'Because I bore him in pain.' Jabez called upon the God of Israel, saying, 'Oh that you would bless me and enlarge my border, and that your hand might be with me, and that you would keep me from harm so that it might not bring me pain!' And God granted what he asked."

Psalm 67:1–3: "May God be gracious to us and bless us and make his face to shine upon us, that [his] way may be known on earth, [his] saving power among all nations. Let the peoples praise you, O God; let all the peoples praise you!"

Pray Alone
- Confession (rest in the forgiveness, cleansing, grace, and mercy of God)
- Praise (look over Psalm 103 and as you read, note particular characteristics of God; then stop and give praise to God for who he is)

1 John 1:9: "If we confess our sins, he is faithful and just to forgive us our sins and to cleanse us from all unrighteousness."

Psalm 103:

"Bless the LORD, O my soul,
    and all that is within me,
      bless his holy name!
Bless the LORD, O my soul,
    and forget not all his benefits,

who forgives all your iniquity,
      who heals all your diseases,
who redeems your life from the pit,
      who crowns you with steadfast love and mercy,
who satisfies you with good
      so that your youth is renewed like the eagle's.

The Lord works righteousness
      and justice for all who are oppressed.
He made known his ways to Moses,
      his acts to the people of Israel.
The Lord is merciful and gracious,
      slow to anger and abounding in steadfast love.
He will not always chide,
      nor will he keep his anger forever.
He does not deal with us according to our sins,
      nor repay us according to our iniquities.
For as high as the heavens are above the earth,
      so great is his steadfast love toward those who fear him;
as far as the east is from the west,
      so far does he remove our transgressions from us.
As a father shows compassion to his children,
      so the Lord shows compassion to those who fear him.
For he knows our frame;
      he remembers that we are dust.

As for man, his days are like grass;
      he flourishes like a flower of the field;
for the wind passes over it, and it is gone,
      and its place knows it no more.
But the steadfast love of the Lord is from everlasting to everlasting on
            those who fear him,
      and his righteousness to children's children,
to those who keep his covenant
      and remember to do his commandments.
The Lord has established his throne in the heavens,
      and his kingdom rules over all.
Bless the Lord, O you his angels,

you mighty ones who do his word,
    obeying the voice of his word!
Bless the LORD, all his hosts,
    his ministers, who do his will!
Bless the LORD, all his works,
    in all places of his dominion.
Bless the LORD, O my soul!"

Pray in Groups
For . . .

- missions internationally
- mission boards
- mission partners
- missionaries
- the persecuted church
- missions nationally
- missions locally

Matthew 9:37–38: "Then he said to his disciples, 'The harvest is plentiful, but the laborers are few; therefore pray earnestly to the Lord of the harvest to send out laborers into his harvest.'"

Pray Together
"Asking amiss is asking from selfish motives. Asking aright has three elements: 1. Desiring God's glory. 2. Confessing our unworthiness and pleading the merits of Jesus. 3. Believing that we do receive the things for which we ask."[1]

In an interview with a man named Parsons, George Müller was asked, "How much time do you spend on your knees?"

"More or less every day," Müller replied. "But I live in the spirit of prayer. I pray as I walk about, when I lie down and when I rise up. And the answers are always coming. Thousands of tens of thousands of times have my prayers been answered. When once I am persuaded that a thing is right and for the glory of God, I go on praying for it until the answer comes."[2]

---

[1]   Roger Steer, *George Müller: Delighted in God* (Fearn, Tain: Scotland: Christian Focus, 2006), 180.
[2]   Müller, quoted in Steer, 223.

- Ask God for blessings. In which of the following arenas do you need a blessing from God?
    - Wisdom
    - Physical
    - Spiritual
    - Financial
    - Relational
    - Lost friends
    - Sick friends
    - Other

James 1:5–6: "If any of you lacks wisdom, let him ask God, who gives generously to all without reproach, and it will be given him. But let him ask in faith, with no doubting, for the one who doubts is like a wave of the sea that is driven and tossed by the wind."

James 4:2–3: "You desire and do not have, so you murder. You covet and cannot obtain, so you fight and quarrel. You do not have, because you do not ask. You ask and do not receive, because you ask wrongly, to spend it on your passions."

Prayer Meeting Template 5

Use these passages and titles to direct prayers.

If you are led to pray, but are not sure what to pray, feel free to pick one of the bullet points below and build upon it.

More importantly, please allow your heart to be sensitive to the Holy Spirit and open to conviction. If any of these elements bring conviction, feel free to confess those shortcomings to God in prayer.

Thanksgiving:

Colossians 1:11–14: "[May you be] strengthened with all power, according to his glorious might, for all endurance and patience with joy, giving thanks to the Father, who has qualified you to share in the inheritance of the saints in light. He has delivered us from the domain of darkness and transferred us to the kingdom of his beloved Son, in whom we have redemption, the forgiveness of sins."

- For what do you have personally to give thanks?
- For what do we have corporately to give thanks?
- What has God done in your life, family, or the life of another that you have seen?
- What material and temporal blessings are you tempted to take for granted?

Salvation:

Romans 10:1: "Brothers, my heart's desire and prayer to God for them is that they may be saved."

Colossians 4:3–4: "At the same time, pray also for us, that God may open to us a door for the word, to declare the mystery of Christ, on account of which I am in prison—that I may make it clear, which is how I ought to speak."

Philemon 5–6: "I hear of your love and of the faith that you have toward the Lord Jesus and for all the saints, and I pray that the sharing of your faith may become effective for the full knowledge of every good thing that is in us for the sake of Christ."

- Who needs the Lord specifically? Pray for your lost friends and family.
- Who needs the Lord generally? Pray for unreached nations and also people groups in: India, China, Pakistan, Bangladesh, Nepal, Indonesia, Laos, Morocco, Iran, etc.
- Pray for the impact of future mission trips.
- Pray for the impact of the missionaries you support.
- Pray for the impact of local Christian agencies.
- Pray for the salvation of the Jewish people (Romans 10–11).
- Pray for the impact of upcoming church events.
- Pray for wisdom on how to personally share the gospel.

Societal Leaders:

1 Timothy 2:1–4: "First of all, then, I urge that supplications, prayers, intercessions, and thanksgivings be made for all people, for kings and all who are in high positions, that we may lead a peaceful and quiet life, godly and dignified in every way. This is good, and it is pleasing in the sight of God our Savior, who desires all people to be saved and to come to the knowledge of the truth."

- upcoming presidential election
- Senate and congressional leaders
- supreme court nominations
- pastors in your church: for their faithfulness, purity, biblical fidelity
- sheriff, city police, fire departments
- city council and mayor
- governor

May all these prayers be answered in accordance with God's will to allow the church to coexist in society peacefully so that the gospel can spread.

General Ministry for All:

Colossians 1:9–11: "And so, from the day we heard, we have not ceased to pray for you, asking that you may be filled with the knowledge of his will in all spiritual wisdom and understanding, so as to walk in a manner worthy of the

Lord, fully pleasing to him, bearing fruit in every good work and increasing in the knowledge of God. May you be strengthened with all power, according to his glorious might, for all endurance and patience with joy."

Colossians 4:12: "Epaphras, who is one of you, a servant of Christ Jesus, greets you, always struggling on your behalf in his prayers, that you may stand mature and fully assured in all the will of God."

1 Thessalonians 5:23: "Now may the God of peace himself sanctify you completely, and may your whole spirit and soul and body be kept blameless at the coming of our Lord Jesus Christ."

2 Thessalonians 3:1–3, 5: "Finally, brothers, pray for us, that the word of the Lord may speed ahead and be honored, as happened among you, and that we may be delivered from wicked and evil men. For not all have faith. But the Lord is faithful. He will establish you and guard you against the evil one. . . . May the Lord direct your hearts to the love of God and to the steadfastness of Christ."

The following can be prayed for our churches, friends, family, selves, coworkers, the sick, anyone . . .

- to be fully assured of God's will and have the strength to walk in it, wisdom in decision-making
- to live out the gospel
- to live faithfully for the glory of God
- to walk in the power of the Spirit of God
- to remove fear and timidity from hearts
- to grow in submission to the Spirit of God and bear fruit giving evidence of God's work
- not to grow weary in doing good
- to have conviction of sin and a desire to walk in holiness
- to walk in the joy of the Lord
- for protection from the attacks of the evil one
- for healing and strength to serve the Lord
- for faithfulness in the midst of difficulty
- for a Christ-centered perspective

Prayer Meeting Template 6

Use these passages and titles to direct prayers.

The following ideas are intended to help guide you through leading one hour of individual and corporate prayer.

15 minutes:

Say, "Meditate on some of these verses and examine your life. Ask God to help you acknowledge his greatness and show you what you need to pray about concerning yourself, your friends, and your family." Then read the following:

Ephesians 1:3, 7–10: "Blessed be the God and Father of our Lord Jesus Christ, who has blessed us in Christ with every spiritual blessing in the heavenly places. . . . In him we have redemption through his blood, the forgiveness of our trespasses, according to the riches of his grace, which he lavished upon us, in all wisdom and insight making known to us the mystery of his will, according to his purpose, which he set forth in Christ as a plan for the fullness of time, to unite all things in him, things in heaven and things on earth."

1 Corinthians 15:58: "Therefore, my beloved brothers, be steadfast, immovable, always abounding in the work of the Lord, knowing that in the Lord your labor is not in vain."

Titus 3:1–2: "Remind them . . . to speak evil of no one, to avoid quarreling, to be gentle, and to show perfect courtesy toward all people."

Philippians 1:27: "Only let your manner of life be worthy of the gospel of Christ."

1 Thessalonians 1:4; 3:12–13: "For we know, brothers loved by God, that he has chosen you. . . . And may the Lord make you increase and abound in love for one another and for all . . . so that he may establish your hearts blameless in holiness before our God and Father, at the coming of our Lord Jesus with all his saints."

15 minutes:

Come back together. Ask whether anyone is willing to share anything the Lord showed them or a specific prayer they were led to pray.

30 minutes:

Say, "Now, we are going to transition into a time of guided corporate prayer. Corporate prayer is to be a unifying time whereby we . . .

- get to share in hearing others intercede before God;
- get to affirm what others are praying;
- get to pray on behalf of others and our church as a whole;
- get to learn from others, what is going on in their lives and how God is directing them; and
- get to symbolize unity.

Corporate prayer was a part of Israel's practice in the Old Testament and the church's practice in the New, and it is our privilege to come together during this time and call out to a holy God." Then read the following verse:

Hebrews 4:15–16: "For we do not have a high priest who is unable to sympathize with our weaknesses, but one who in every respect has been tempted as we are, yet without sin. Let us then with confidence draw near to the throne of grace, that we may receive mercy and find grace to help in time of need."

Pray for Your Church's Guests:
Matthew 6:33: "But seek first the kingdom of God and his righteousness, and all these things will be added to you."

Pray for Your Church's People:
Ephesians 4:1–3: "I therefore, a prisoner for the Lord, urge you to walk in a manner worthy of the calling to which you have been called, with all humility and gentleness, with patience, bearing with one another in love, eager to maintain the unity of the Spirit in the bond of peace."

Pray for Your Pastors, Deacons, and Staff:
Ephesians 4:4–7, 11–14: "There is one body and one Spirit—just as you were called to the one hope that belongs to your call—one Lord, one faith, one baptism, one God and Father of all, who is over all and through all and in

all. But grace was given to each one of us according to the measure of Christ's gift. . . . And he gave the apostles, the prophets, the evangelists, the shepherds and teachers, to equip the saints for the work of ministry, for building up the body of Christ, until we all attain to the unity of the faith and of the knowledge of the Son of God, to mature manhood, to the measure of the stature of the fullness of Christ, so that we may no longer be children, tossed to and fro by the waves and carried about by every wind of doctrine, by human cunning, by craftiness in deceitful schemes."

Pray for Your Church's Children, Youth, and College Students:
2 Peter 3:17–18: "You therefore, beloved, knowing this beforehand, take care that you are not carried away with the error of lawless people and lose your own stability. But grow in the grace and knowledge of our Lord and Savior Jesus Christ. To him be the glory both now and to the day of eternity. Amen."

Prayer Meeting Template 7

Use these passages and titles to direct prayers.

P: I want to praise God for . . .

R: I want to repent of . . .

A: I want to ask God for . . .

Y: I yield my desires to his ultimate will.

Why prayer?

- Because of the example of Christ

Hebrews 5:7: "In the days of his flesh, Jesus offered up prayers and supplications, with loud cries and tears, to him who was able to save him from death, and he was heard because of his reverence."

- Because it is commanded

Romans 12:12: "Rejoice in hope, be patient in tribulation, be constant in prayer."

- Because it's the means by which God often accomplishes his will (it makes a difference)

James 1:5: "If any of you lacks wisdom, let him ask God, who gives generously to all without reproach, and it will be given him."

However, the way we live matters and impacts our prayers.

1 Peter 3:7: "Likewise, husbands, live with your wives in an understanding way, showing honor to the woman as the weaker vessel, since they are heirs with you of the grace of life, so that your prayers may not be hindered."

1 Peter 4:7: "The end of all things is at hand; therefore be self-controlled and sober-minded for the sake of your prayers."

P: Psalm 100:1–5: "Make a joyful noise to the LORD, all the earth! Serve the LORD with gladness! Come into his presence with singing! Know that the LORD, he is God! It is he who made us, and we are his; we are his people, and the sheep of his pasture. Enter his gates with thanksgiving, and his courts with praise! Give thanks to him; bless his name! For the LORD is good; his steadfast love endures forever, and his faithfulness to all generations."

R: Psalm 103:1–12: "Bless the LORD, O my soul, and all that is within me, bless his holy name! Bless the LORD, O my soul, and forget not all his benefits, who forgives all your iniquity, who heals all your diseases, who redeems your life from the pit, who crowns you with steadfast love and mercy, who satisfies you with good so that your youth is renewed like the eagle's. The LORD works righteousness and justice for all who are oppressed. He made known his ways to Moses, his acts to the people of Israel. The LORD is merciful and gracious, slow to anger and abounding in steadfast love. He will not always chide, nor will he keep his anger forever. He does not deal with us according to our sins, nor repay us according to our iniquities. For as high as the heavens are above the earth, so great is his steadfast love toward those who fear him; as far as the east is from the west, so far does he remove our transgressions from us."

A: Psalm 4:1: "Answer me when I call, O God of my righteousness! You have given me relief when I was in distress. Be gracious to me and hear my prayer!"

Y: Psalm 69:13: "But as for me, my prayer is to you, O Lᴏʀᴅ. At an acceptable time, O God, in the abundance of your steadfast love answer me in your saving faithfulness."

SCRIPTURE INDEX